TIME FOR ARISTOTLE

OXFORD ARISTOTLE STUDIES

General Editors
Julia Annas and Lindsay Judson

PUBLISHED IN THE SERIES

Aristotle on Meaning and Essence
David Charles

Time for Aristotle
Physics IV. 10–14
Ursula Coope

Aristotle on Teleology
Monte Ransome Johnson

On Location
Aristotle's Concept of Place
Benjamin Morison

Order in Multiplicity
Homonymy in the Philosophy of Aristotle
Christopher Shields

Aristotle's Theory of Substance
The Categories *and* Metaphysics *Zeta*
Michael V. Wedin

Aristotle's *De Interpretatione*
Contradiction and Dialectic
C. W. A. Whitaker

Time for Aristotle

Physics IV.10–14

URSULA COOPE

CLARENDON PRESS • OXFORD

OXFORD

UNIVERSITY PRESS

Great Clarendon Street, Oxford OX2 6DP

Oxford University Press is a department of the University of Oxford.
It furthers the University's objective of excellence in research, scholarship,
and education by publishing worldwide in

Oxford New York

Auckland Cape Town Dar es Salaam Hong Kong Karachi
Kuala Lumpur Madrid Melbourne Mexico City Nairobi
New Delhi Shanghai Taipei Toronto

With offices in

Argentina Austria Brazil Chile Czech Republic France Greece
Guatemala Hungary Italy Japan Poland Portugal Singapore
South Korea Switzerland Thailand Turkey Ukraine Vietnam

Oxford is a registered trade mark of Oxford University Press
in the UK and in certain other countries

Published in the United States
by Oxford University Press Inc., New York

First published 2005

British Library Cataloguing in Publication Data
Data available

Library of Congress Cataloging in Publication Data
Data available

Typeset by SPI Publisher Services, Pondicherry, India

Printed in Great Britain
on acid-free paper by
Biddles Ltd, Kings Lynn, Norfolk

ISBN 0-19-924790-0   ISBN 978-0-19-924790-5

1 3 5 7 9 10 8 6 4 2

To Nicholas,
who was just starting out in philosophy

atque in perpetuum, frater, ave atque vale

Preface

This book is a much revised version of my Ph.D. dissertation. It is a product not only of my own efforts, but also of the help and advice I have received, over the years, from others. Above all, I would like to thank Sarah Broadie. My interest in Aristotle's discussion of time stems from a graduate seminar of hers on *Physics* III–IV. Without her, it is unlikely that I would have written either the book or the dissertation. She has read and commented on every draft, and has from first to last been a source of encouragement, helpful criticisms, and interesting suggestions.

I was also very lucky to be able to work with Alan Code at Berkeley, when I was in the final stages of writing the dissertation. I discussed each chapter with him as I wrote it, and benefited a great deal from his ability to come up with arguments in defence of my position, at a time when I could only see what appeared to be devastating objections to it. Though I only worked with him for a short time, the book is very much better as a result. I would also like to thank Tony Long, who, as one of my examiners, read the final version of the dissertation and made several helpful comments on it.

A number of people, besides those named above, have read and commented on drafts of all or part of the book. Between them, they have saved me from many blunders and confusions. My particular thanks, for this, go to Verity Harte, Bob Heinaman, Philip Hunter, Jonathan Lear, and Ben Morison. Edward Hussey, who read the book for OUP, wrote pages of detailed comments, full of interesting and constructive criticisms, and an anonymous referee for OUP also made many helpful suggestions for improvement. I would also like to thank Peter Momtchiloff of OUP for his helpfulness and for his patience in the face of many missed deadlines.

Most of the work for my dissertation was done during the three years I spent as a visiting graduate student at Princeton. I would like to thank the Philosophy Department there, and especially the members of the ancient philosophy program, for providing such a friendly and intellectually stimulating environment. I was particularly fortunate to be there at the same time as my fellow students, Jonathan Beere, Zena Hitz, and Gabriel Richardson-Lear. Many of the ideas in this book were developed in conversations with them, and their friendship was a great support to me in very difficult times.

The work of turning the dissertation into a book was mostly carried out in London, first of all as a Jacobsen Fellow at University College and, more recently, as a lecturer at Birkbeck. I am grateful to my colleagues and students in London for helping to make it such a wonderful place to study philosophy. Much of the material in the book was presented as part of a graduate seminar I gave at Princeton, when I was a visiting assistant professor there in 2003. I thank the participants in that seminar for much interesting discussion. Thanks are due also to Princeton for inviting me, and to my Birkbeck colleagues for allowing me to take up the offer. I have presented papers based on drafts of parts of the book to audiences at the Cambridge B-Club, the Northern Association of Ancient Philosophy, the UCL Department of Science and Technology Studies, and to the philosophy departments at Birkbeck, Bristol, Princeton, Sheffield, and St Andrews. I am grateful for the many interesting comments and questions I received on these occasions.

Finally, many thanks to my parents, Christopher Coope and Jennifer Jackson, for all their support and encouragement over the years, and to my husband, Philip Hunter, for making the final stages of writing the book so extraordinarily happy. *Time for Aristotle* is dedicated to my younger brother, Nicholas, who died climbing in Glen Clova, when he was just about to embark on a philosophy degree at St Andrews.

Contents

Introduction

Aristotle's account of time is part of his *Physics*. Physics is the study of natural things, of those things that have a nature (*phusis*). For a thing to have a nature is for it to have an inner source of changing and of staying the same. An oak tree, for instance, has a nature; a bed does not. The oak tree has certain characteristic ways of changing: it loses its leaves in autumn, it grows acorns, it puts out roots of a certain shape. According to Aristotle, these characteristic changes are not caused purely by the tree's environment or by the stuff of which the tree is made.[1] Though they require certain background environmental conditions (water, sunlight, and so on), they are changes that the oak tree undergoes of itself: the primary reason why it changes in these ways is that it is an oak tree. In contrast, a bed does not have characteristic ways of changing. There are no changes that it undergoes of itself in virtue of being a bed. Its changes are caused partly by its environment and partly by the stuff of which it is made. If we bury a bed and its rotting frame puts out shoots, this will be because it is wooden, not because it is an ex-bed. The bed will not spawn baby beds.

Living things all have natures. So also do Aristotle's four 'simple bodies': earth, air, fire, and water, each of which has a natural tendency to occupy a particular place in the universe (the earth at the centre, then, in concentric circles, water, air, and fire). Physics, then, is the study of these things.[2]

---

[1] Any particular oak tree will also undergo other changes that *are* caused primarily by its environment. For example, if the tree is struck by lightning, it will burn; if we take a saw to its branches, they will fall off.

[2] Aristotle lays out his account of nature in *Physics* II. The example of a bed was originally from the philosopher Antiphon, who did not make Aristotle's distinction between natural and artificial things, but instead used this example to argue that the nature of a thing is the stuff of which it is made (*Physics* II.1.193^{a}9–17).

That such a science is possible is not something Aristotle can just take for granted. He is writing against a Platonic background. Plato and his followers in the Academy held that the most fundamental kinds of being were unchanging and imperceptible: forms, like the One and the Good, or (for those under the influence of Pythagoras) numbers. This raises a question about the status of changing, perceptible things: can there be any systematic study of such things? Plato's own discussion of physical phenomena, in the *Timaeus*, is presented as an *eikos muthos*, a likely tale.[3] Aristotle wants to show that physics can be a genuine science. It is possible to have a systematic body of knowledge of such things as oak trees, giraffes, buttercups, and spiders.[4]

He argues, in the *Categories*, that the basic kinds of being, the *primary substances*, are not Platonic forms but rather particular persisting things, like this man and this horse. One of the distinctive characteristics of primary substances is that they can stay the same through change.[5] If there is knowledge of anything, there must be knowledge of substances, so this claim in the *Categories* already implies that there can be a science of changing things. But it is in the *Physics* that he does the most to put this science on a firm footing. It is there that he explains what it is for something to have a nature and distinguishes those things that happen by nature from those things that happen by accident.[6] He also argues in the *Physics* that if there is to be change at all, there must be certain imperishable things that are forever in motion. The unending and uniform rotation of the heavenly bodies (the planets and the stars) provides a necessary backdrop to the intermittent and various changes that we see around us.[7]

In the section of the *Physics* that will chiefly concern us, he lays out his accounts of four things that are fundamental to the study of nature: change, the infinite, place, and time.[8] Since nature is a source of change,

---

[3] *Timaeus* 29b–d.
[4] Indeed, a significant portion of his output is a monumental attempt to gather and record facts about the physiology of different kinds of living thing. (See, for instance, his *History of Animals* and *Parts of Animals*.)
[5] *Categories* 5.4^{a}10–11.
[6] There is, he says, no science of the accidental (*Metaphysics* VI.2.1027^{a}19–20).
[7] He defends this claim in *Physics* VIII.
[8] *Physics* III and IV. He also discusses the void. At the beginning of *Physics* III.1, he says that it is generally thought (*dokei*) that change is infinitely divisible and that there can only be change if there are place, time, and void (III.1.200^{b}16–21). It later emerges

in order to understand what it is to have a nature we need an account of change. Changes, Aristotle thinks, are infinitely divisible, so in providing a foundation for physics, we must tackle the obscure notion of the infinite. He provides an account of place, because if there is to be any kind of change there must be change of place.[9] And an account of time is also needed, since 'all changes and all changing things are in time' ($222^{b}30-1$).[10]

This explains the role that the account of time plays in Aristotle's overall system. If we are to understand his physics as a whole, we need to grapple with his difficult remarks about time. But are these remarks of more than historical interest? Do they have something important to say to a modern philosopher who is interested in the notions of time and change? My contention is that they do, but that the way in which they do is rather indirect.

A modern philosopher who reads Aristotle's discussion of time will find that, though it is expressed in language that is frustratingly obscure and elliptical, the questions it addresses seem relatively familiar. Aristotle starts out by puzzling over whether time can be something that is, given that neither the past nor the future is. This calls to mind the arguments of those modern philosophers who call themselves 'presentists' and claim that everything that exists is present.[11] He goes on to argue that the present, or 'now', is something that in a way remains always the same, but is also always different. This is often taken to show that he thinks the now is something that moves, a view much criticized and occasionally defended in modern philosophy.[12] He discusses time's relation to change and to the mind, arguing that both change and (more

that he endorses all of this generally accepted view except for the claim that there can only be change if there is void. In his discussion of void he argues, not only that there can be change in the absence of void, but that it is, in fact, impossible for there to be void (IV.6–9).

[9] As I have said, for there to be change, the heavenly bodies must engage in eternal movement (that is, change of place). Moreover, whenever one thing acts on another to produce a change, there must be spatial movement, since before one thing can act on another, the thing that acts and the thing that is acted upon must approach one another (*Physics* VIII.7).

[10] As we shall see, Aristotle later qualifies this claim. He thinks that there is a sense in which things that are in everlasting motion are not in time (see below, Ch. 9).

[11] Presentism is defended, for instance by Bigelow (1996).

[12] The moving-now view is defended by Schlesinger (1982). It is criticized by Williams (1951) and Smart (1949) (among others).

surprisingly) mind are necessary preconditions for the existence of time. Whether or not there can be time without change is a question central to certain modern debates about the reducibility of facts about time to facts about things in time.[13] Finally, he gives an account of what he calls the 'before and after in time' in terms of its relation to a more basic kind of before and after order: the before and after in change. It is easy to be reminded here of reductive theories, such as causal theories of time, that attempt to explain temporal asymmetry in terms of some other, more basic kind of asymmetry.[14]

However, this appearance of familiarity is, I think, largely deceptive. For the most part, the questions Aristotle addresses here are different from those raised in modern discussions. When he puzzles over whether time can be something that is, he is not considering the presentist view that nothing can exist except what is at the present. Unlike the presentist, his puzzle is solely about *time*, not about things that are *in time*. He never suggests that there is a difficulty about how things, like changes, that are in time can extend beyond the present. Moreover, in his remarks about the sameness of the now, he is not describing the now as something that moves. The claim that earlier and later nows are in some way the same is, instead, bound up with an aspect of his account that is, to us, distinctly odd: his view that time is a kind of number. He holds that the sameness of earlier and later nows is a necessary condition of their countability. Finally, in spite of its concern with order and asymmetry, Aristotle's account turns out to have little in common with modern reductive explanations of temporal order. That this is so is brought out, among other things, by his readiness to take for granted the notion of simultaneity. He thinks it important to argue that simultaneous changes are all at one and the same time, but he sees no need to explain in virtue of what certain changes are simultaneous. He simply assumes the existence of this relation between changes, as if it is something basic and inexplicable.

It follows that the interest of Aristotle's account does not lie in its ability to provide answers to the questions modern philosophers ask about time. It rarely even addresses these questions. Its interest stems instead from the fact that the questions that trouble him are so different

[13] For a discussion of this, see Newton-Smith (1980: ch. 2). Newton-Smith calls the reductionist assumption that there can be no time without change 'Aristotle's Principle'.
[14] Mellor defends such a theory. (See Mellor 1998: ch. 10 and 11).

from those that naturally occur to us. The challenge to the interpreter is to understand why these are the questions Aristotle considers important. If we can understand this, we shall gain a new perspective on our own thinking about time. We can shed light on our own assumptions by thinking ourselves into the position of someone who does not share them. By asking why Aristotle thought certain questions but not others important, we can better understand our own presuppositions about which questions are central in the philosophy of time. And as we shall see, the questions he asks are also interesting in their own right.

I shall argue that Aristotle's account represents time as a kind of universal order and that this is why he defines it, oddly, as a number. It is, he says, a 'number of change', a single order within which all changes are related to one another. He argues that the existence of this single order depends on the existence of beings, like us, who can count. It depends on the fact that we count *nows* in a certain way. To count a now is to mark a dividing-point in all the changes that are going on at it. Our counting thus introduces a kind of uniformity into the world. It allows us to delimit, within a change, arbitrary parts that are exactly simultaneous to corresponding parts in every other change that is going on. As we shall see, one of Aristotle's central concerns is to explain how time can have this kind of uniformity. He asks what account of time will make sense of the fact that 'though changes are various and separate from one another, time is everywhere the same' (223^{b}10–11).

Before we can begin to understand these claims, we need to have some familiarity with Aristotle's views on two closely related subjects. We need to look at his account of change and at his remarks about the sense in which change is divisible.

THE ACCOUNT OF CHANGE

In defining time as a number of change, Aristotle assumes that change is, in an important sense, prior to time. Time is something that is essentially dependent on change, and because of this, a true understanding of time must draw upon a prior understanding of change. This implies that change itself can be defined in a way that makes no reference to time. It thus rules out a certain natural way of using the notion of time to define change. Aristotle could not, for instance, go along with Bertrand Russell's claim that the concept of motion (or change of place) is 'logically subsequent to that of occupying a place at a time'. Nor could he accept Russell's definition of motion as 'the occupation, by one entity, of a continuous series of places at a continuous series of times'.[15] What, then, is Aristotle's account of change? Can he avoid making the nature of change essentially dependent on that of time?

He lays out his account of change in books I and III of the *Physics*. He explains first, in Book I, that change always involves an underlying thing and two contraries.[16] The underlying thing persists through the change, losing one contrary and gaining the other. For instance, when a man becomes musical, the underlying thing is the man. He persists through the change, being first unmusical and then musical.

This tells us something about the basic structure of a change, but a full account of change must invoke the notion of potentiality. For such an account, we need to turn to *Physics* III.1–2. Aristotle says there that change is 'the actuality (*entelecheia*) of that which potentially is, *qua* such' (201ª10–11). What does this rather cryptic formula mean?[17]

The notions of potentiality and actuality that Aristotle employs in this definition figure centrally in much of his thinking about metaphysics. Unfortunately, they are notoriously difficult to understand. His thought here seems to be this. If something is changing, it must be

---

[15] B. Russell (1937: 469).

[16] *Physics* I.7–9.

[17] The interpretation I give is defended by Kosman (1969), Broadie (1982a: ch. 3 part 1) and Hussey (1993: 58–62). There are at least two alternative ways in which this formula has been taken. Kostman (1987) argues that the word *entelecheia*, which I have translated 'actuality' here, should really be translated 'actualization'. On his view, Aristotle is saying that change is the actualization of what is potentially in a certain end state F, *qua* potentially in that end state F. (One disadvantage of this view is that it makes the *qua* clause redundant.) Heinaman (1994) argues that the potential referred to in the definition is not the potential to be in the end state but rather the potential to be changing. On his view, then, Aristotle is saying that change is the actuality of what is potentially changing *qua* potentially changing. Both of these interpretations give Aristotle an account of change that is circular (the first, because it defines change in terms of a kind of actualization, or *process* of becoming actual; the second, because it defines change as the actuality of a potential to be *changing*). But, of course, whether this is a decisive objection depends on Aristotle's aims in giving this account. Is he trying to give a definition of change in terms of other concepts, or is he merely explaining further what is involved in a change (telling us, for instance, that change always involves a potential of a certain kind)?

changing towards some particular end state. For there to be a change, there must be something that exists before the change and that has the potential to be in the end state of the change. Consider, for example, the change that is the coming-to-be of a statue. For this change to occur, there must be some stuff (some bronze, perhaps) that is not (yet) a statue but has the potential to be a statue. When Aristotle writes of 'that which potentially is', he is referring to that which is potentially in the end state of the change. For instance, in our example, 'that which potentially is' is the bronze and the potential that the bronze has is the potential to be a statue.

Aristotle's claim is that the bronze is changing into a statue just in case its potential to be a statue is, in a certain sense, actual.[18] This notion of a potential's being actual is almost impossible to explain without resorting to metaphor. The idea is that until the change begins, the bronze's potential to be a statue is lying dormant. When the bronze is becoming a statue, its potential to be a statue makes a difference to *what is actually happening* (whereas before, it only made a difference to what *might* happen).

According to Aristotle's definition, the change is 'the actuality of that which potentially is, *qua* such'. In our example, the change into a statue is an actuality of the bronze (which is potentially a statue). What, though, is the meaning of the addition '*qua* such'? Aristotle draws a distinction between the actuality of the bronze *in so far as it is just bronze* and the actuality of the bronze *in so far as it is potentially a statue*. He wants to say that it is only the latter kind of actuality that is a change. The actuality of the bronze in so far as it is just bronze is simply: being bronze. *Being bronze* is not a way of changing. The actuality that is the change is the actuality of the bronze *qua* potentially being something else. The bronze's change into a statue is the actuality of the bronze *qua* potentially being a statue (201ᵃ29–ᵇ5).

This leaves us with one obvious difficulty. It might seem that the bronze's potential to be a statue is most fully actual when the statue exists in its finished state. But at that point the change we are trying to define is already over: the bronze is no longer becoming a statue. Given that he wants to define change as the actuality of a potential to be in

---

[18] Indeed, he wants to say that the bronze's change into a statue *just is* an actuality of the bronze's potential to be a statue.

some end state, how can Aristotle distinguish between *changing into* that state and *statically being in* that state? How, in our example, can he distinguish between becoming a statue and simply being a statue?

To answer this, it is necessary to think once more about the significance of the '*qua*' clause in the definition. We have already invoked this clause in order to distinguish *becoming a statue* from *being bronze*. As we have seen, the change is the actuality of the bronze *qua* potentially a statue (not simply *qua* potentially bronze). In order to distinguish *becoming a statue* from *being a statue*, we need to spell out the phrase '*qua* such' in a way that adds a further emphasis. The change in question is the actuality of the bronze *qua potentially (but not actually)* a statue. Aristotle explains that, as he is using the notion of 'potential' here, something only counts as potentially F, when it is not in fact F. When the statue has been made, the bronze is no longer something that is (in this sense) 'potentially a statue'. Or, as he puts it (using a different example), 'when the house is, the buildable [i.e. what is potentially but not actually a house] no longer is' (201^{b}11). Change is the actuality of something that is, in this way, merely potential. When something is becoming F, its potential to be F is *as actual as is compatible with merely being a potential*. Though *being a statue* is a kind of actuality of the bronze, it is not the actuality of the bronze's potential to be a statue, considered as a *mere* potential. *Becoming a statue* is the actuality of the bronze in so far as it is potentially, but only potentially, a statue. That is to say, it is 'the actuality of that which potentially is, *qua* such' (201^{a}10–11).[19]

From this account it follows that change is, in a certain sense, incomplete. 'Change is held to be a kind of actuality, but an incomplete

---

[19] A full defence of Aristotle's account would have to show that it can, in *every* instance, correctly distinguish between *changing* and *being at rest*. There are several apparent difficulties that such a defence would need to address. For example, suppose that I am trying without success to raise my arm and that the reason for my lack of success is that someone else is holding my arm down. In this case, there is a sense in which I am using my potential to raise my arm, though my arm is not going up. If my arm were free, it would rise. It is tempting to say of such a case that the potential I have for raising my arm is *actual in so far as it is merely potential*. But of course no *change* is occurring: I am not in fact raising my arm. Again, consider the case of someone who rests for a while in the middle of a journey to his final destination. He has, while he is resting, a potential to be at his final destination, and this potential is actual in a way that it was not actual before the movement began. But for all that, he is resting, rather than moving towards his destination. To defend his account, Aristotle would need to distinguish *these* ways in which a potential can be actual from the way that the potential that governs a change is actual while that change is going on.

one. The reason is that the potential of which it is the actuality is incomplete' (201ᵇ31–3). The sense in which the potential is incomplete is that it is a potential a thing has to be something that it is not. The bronze's potential to be a statue is only actual-*qua*-potential when it is not yet a statue.

For our purposes, there are several aspects of this account of change that are important. First, Aristotle explains change in terms of the notions of potentiality and actuality. His account makes no explicit reference to time. That there should be such an account of change is, as I have said, presupposed by his whole project of explaining time in terms of its relation to change. Second, a change is, in a certain sense, asymmetric. It is defined in terms of a potential to be in some *end* state. As Hussey puts it, 'a change "points forward" to its completion in a way in which it does not "point backward" to its inception'.[20] This might suggest that the account of change does, after all, make essential reference to time. However, as we shall see, Aristotle's view is that this asymmetry within changes is itself basic. It is temporal asymmetry that depends on the asymmetries within changes, rather than vice versa. Finally, this definition of change provides Aristotle with the resources to make sense of a certain kind of interference. The acorn is changing into an oak tree. But this change may or may not result in there actually being an oak tree. If the young sapling is eaten by wild animals, the oak tree never materializes, but it is nevertheless true that the acorn was *becoming an oak* and not *becoming a sapling*. This is because the potential that governed the acorn's change was the potential to be an oak tree and not the potential to be a sapling. The change was the actuality of the potential oak tree, *qua* potentially an oak tree. This final feature of change is, as I later argue, the key to an analogy Aristotle draws between change and spatial magnitude.

DIVISIONS IN TIME AND IN CHANGE

In his account of time, Aristotle takes for granted certain views about the sense in which boundaries, or divisions, can exist within a continuum. These views are partly motivated by his need to reconcile two claims about the infinite. On the one hand, he thinks that continuous things,

---

[20] Hussey (1993: xiv).

like lines, changes, and time, are infinitely divisible. On the other, he argues that there is no actual infinite: it is not possible for infinitely many things to exist all at once; nor can anything ever have completed infinitely many changes.[21]

These two claims might seem incompatible. If a line is infinitely divisible, then surely its infinitely many parts are things that all exist at once. To complete an infinitely divisible change is, surely, to complete infinitely many subchanges. Aristotle defends his account of the infinite by denying these natural assumptions. He argues instead that a line, though infinitely divisible, is not composed of infinitely many actual parts. More generally, from the fact that something is infinitely divisible it does not follow that there are, in actuality, infinitely many parts into which it might be divided.

To make sense of this, he again invokes the notion of potentiality. When we cut a line in two, we create two actual line-parts and the points that bound them. A line has the potential to be indefinitely divided. However many parts we create by dividing the line, we could (at least in theory) always make more. In this sense, there are *potentially* infinitely many parts in the line and infinitely many points to bound them.

It is important to be clear about what this means. To say that there are potentially infinitely many parts or points in a line is not to say that the line has, in it, infinitely many *potential parts* or *potential points*.[22] For Aristotle, a line is not composed of infinitely many *anythings*, be they potential or actual. If it were, then paradox would result. For instance, the infinite collection of potential points in a particular line would have parts that were also infinite collections (e.g. the collection of potential points in half of the line). But Aristotle has already argued that it is

---

[21] He develops his account of the infinite in *Physics* III.4–8. The view that infinitely many distinct tasks cannot ever have been completed is presupposed by his reply to Zeno in *Physics* VIII.8.263^{a}4–^{b}9.

[22] When Aristotle says (at *Physics* VIII.8.263^{b}5–6) that it is possible to traverse infinitely many things that are 'in potentiality but not in actuality', he does not mean that it is possible to traverse infinitely many potential things. Rather, it is possible to traverse something that has the potential to be divided into infinitely many things. (The revised Oxford translation of Hardie and Gaye (Barnes 1984) is, I think, misleading here. It has: 'if the units are actual, it is not possible; if they are potential, it is possible'.) Similarly, when he says, at 263^{a}28–9, that 'in what is continuous there are infinitely many halves in potentiality, not in actuality' he does not mean (as the revised Oxford translation has it) that what is continuous contains an infinite number of halves that 'are not actual but potential halves'.

impossible for something to be composed of infinite parts.[23] For the line to be infinitely divisible is for there to be no limit to the number of divisions that *could be made* in it, not for it to contain an unlimited number of *makeable divisions*.

What, then, is involved in dividing something continuous into parts? On Aristotle's view, we can only divide something into two by creating in it two boundaries: one boundary for each of the two parts. There are two different ways to create a double division of this sort in a line. One way is physically to cut the line in two, so that the two parts are separate from each other and each of them has its own boundaries. The other way is to move over the line, stopping when we are part way through the movement. By stopping at a certain point on a line and then starting out from that point, we create a double boundary. When we stop and then start at a point, we treat the point as two, allowing it to serve both as a boundary of the part to one side of it and as a boundary of the part to the other side. To do this is to create an actual division in the line.[24] Making an actual division in a change is less straightforward. To make an actual division in the middle of the change, we would need to find some way to treat one and the same instantaneous change-stage as a double boundary: both as the end of the part of the change that comes before it and as a beginning of the part that is to come. Aristotle argues that the only way to divide a change in this way is to interrupt it. There are, thus, no actual divisions in an uninterrupted change.[25] Time is even

---

[23] *Physics* III.5.204ᵃ20–7. This point is noted by Sorabji (1983: 211–12), who defends the interpretation I am putting forward here.

[24] See *Physics* IV.11.220ᵃ12–13: 'when one takes the point in this way, treating one point as two, it is necessary to come to a stop, if the same point is to be both a beginning and an end'. See also Aristotle's discussion in *Physics* VIII.8.262ᵃ12–263ᵇ9. He explains there that a point that divides a line is one in number but two in definition (since it is an end of one part of the line and a beginning of the other). Any point between the two extremes on the line is potentially such a division, but 'it is not actually so, unless something divides the line by coming to a halt at that point and then starting to move again. In this way, the middle point becomes both a beginning and an end: a beginning of the latter part and an end of the first part' (262ᵃ22–6).

[25] On this, see again *Physics* VIII.8.262ᵃ12–263ᵇ9. Aristotle argues, for this reason, that it is impossible for something that is thrown upwards to a point D to turn back on itself and move downwards, unless it pauses at D. *Being at D* would, he thinks, be an actual division in this up-and-down movement. But the movement can only be actually divided at D if the moving thing stops at D (so that being at D serves first as the end point of the upwards movement and then as the starting point of the downwards movement) (262ᵇ22–263ᵃ2).

less subject to division than change. In time, there are no actual divisions. We cannot interrupt time, separating it into two parts with something other than time between them.[26]

These views about what it takes for there to be an actual division in a thing raise questions about how time, or even change, can be said to have parts at all. If we can only divide a change into separate parts by interrupting it, then how can an uninterrupted change have parts? If it is impossible to make an actual division in time, then how can there be any parts in time?

Aristotle's answer, I think, is that we can create parts in a thing without actually dividing it. We do this by marking a *potential* division. I have already denied that continua like time and change have, in them, infinitely many potential divisions. What is true, though, is that a potential division *could be created* anywhere in a continuum. Though a line does not contain infinitely many points, I can mark out, and hence create, a point anywhere on it. In doing this, I am creating a potential division: a point at which I *could* cut the line into two and then separate the parts. Similarly, I can make a potential division in a change. To do this, I mark out an instant of the change (say, by 'counting' that instant). The instant I mark is a potential division, since it is a point at which the change could be interrupted. Finally, it is also possible to make a potential division in time. To make such a division, it is necessary to mark out the now, the indivisible boundary between the present and the future. The now is not, of course, a point at which time could actually be divided: we cannot separate the time on one side of the now from the time on the other side of it. As Aristotle says, it only 'divides potentially' (222ᵃ14). Nevertheless, just as marking potential divisions in a line creates parts in the line, so also marking nows creates parts in time. The difference is just that the parts of the line could

---

[26] He explains this difference between time and a line at *Physics* IV.11.220ᵃ10–16 and also at IV.13.222ᵃ12–20. At 222ᵃ14, he says that the now only divides time *potentially*. It cannot be an actual division in time (as a point can be an actual division on a line) as it is not possible for something to come to a halt at the now, and then start moving again from the very same now. For this reason, we cannot make a now into what I have been calling a double boundary, in the way that we make a point on a line into a double boundary.

actually be divided from each other, whereas the parts of time could not be.[27]

These, then, are Aristotle's views about continua and their parts. There are three lessons from all this that we will need to bear in mind when we look at the account of time. First, for Aristotle, indivisible things like points and instants exist only in so far as they are boundaries, divisions, or potential divisions, of a continuum. They are, thus, essentially dependent entities. A boundary must always be a boundary *of* something or other. Second, for a boundary to be (and hence for the part it bounds to be), it must be marked out in some way from its surroundings. A continuous thing that contains no such boundaries will not contain any parts (although it will, of course, be divisible). Third, when I mark a now I create a potential division, both in time and in whatever changes are then going on. It is thus by marking nows that we create parts in time and in changes.

---

[27] There is, of course, something odd about the claim that there can be potential but not actual divisions in time. In what sense is a division a potential division if it is not even possible that it could be an actual division? I suspect that in thinking of time in this way, Aristotle is making use of an analogy between time and a line. He calls a now a 'potential division' because it is marked out from time just as a potential division of a line is marked out from the line.

PART I

INTRODUCTORY PUZZLES AND THE STARTING POINTS OF INQUIRY

1

The Introductory Puzzles

Aristotle introduces his account of time with three puzzles. The puzzles suggest, he says, either that there is no such thing as time or that time has a shadowy kind of existence: it is 'barely and scarcely'. He must have some answer to these puzzles. After all, he goes on to give an account of time. But he never tells us explicitly what his answer is.

This failure to provide a solution is striking. It is common Aristotelian practice to start out a discussion by going through various puzzles. His account of place begins with puzzles about place (IV.1.209^{a}2 ff.). His account of the infinite opens with a series of arguments for and against the existence of something infinite (III. 4–5). In each of these cases, he ends by returning to the initial puzzles and attempting to show how his account can solve them.[1] In contrast, it is typical of the elliptical and compressed nature of his remarks on time that they leave the reader guessing what the solution to the initial puzzles might be. Does the fact that time, on Aristotle's view, is something dependent on change allow us to answer the puzzles? Should we look for the solution in Aristotle's brief remarks about the relation between time and the soul? Or is it to be found in his lengthy and difficult discussion of the now?

Whatever their ultimate solution, these puzzles draw attention to two questions that will be important in Aristotle's account. What kind of a being is time? And what is its relation to the present, or 'now'? More specifically, the puzzles invite us to think critically about one of our natural ways of picturing time. It is natural to picture time as a line, with the now as a point on the line. For Aristotle, there is something right

---

[1] The arguments that there is an actual infinite are answered in *Physics* III.8. Aristotle explicitly returns to the puzzles about place in IV.5.212^{b}22 ff. It is worth noting, however, that though he claims that his account of place solves 'all the puzzles' (212^{b}22–3), he only goes on to provide explicit solutions to some of them. See Ross (1936: 564, ad. 209^{a}2–30).

about this picture. Time, like a line, is continuous and the now, like a point, is indivisible. But these initial puzzles place some strain on this picture of time. They do this in two ways. First, there is some sense in which the now is all that there is of time (the now is what *is*, whereas the rest of time either was or will be), but it is hard to see how a point could be all that there was of a line. Second, the nows seem to exist in succession, one after another, but it is hard to make sense of this if (as Aristotle thinks) time, like a line, is infinitely divisible. If any two nows are separated by a divisible period of time, then one now cannot immediately succeed another. Though he does not provide any explicit solution to the initial puzzles, Aristotle does, later in his account, have something positive to say about the ways in which time is or is not like a line. I shall return to his remarks about this in Chapter 8, below, when I discuss his views on the now.

THE FIRST TWO PUZZLES: IT SEEMS
THAT NONE OF TIME IS

Aristotle starts out with two puzzles that are closely related. The first arises because time consists of the future (which is not yet) and the past (which is no longer). This seems to imply that no part of time *is*. Time is made up wholly of things that either were or will be. But how can something exist if no part of it exists?

One part of it has been and is not, another part of it will be and is not yet. From these are composed both the infinite and whatever time is on any given occasion taken. But what is composed of non-beings might seem to be incapable of participating in being (*metechein ousias*). $(217^{b}33–218^{a}3)^{2}$

The second puzzle complements the first. In reply to the first puzzle someone might say that there is a part of time that exists, namely the present, or 'now'. In the second puzzle Aristotle anticipates this objection and claims that the now is not a part of time. When divisible things exist, he says, either one or more of their parts must exist. But no part of time exists. The now is not a part.

---

[2] Translations are my own, but I have greatly benefited from the use of Hussey (1993).

In the case of anything divisible, if it is, it is necessary that when it is, either all or some of its parts must exist. But of time, though it is divisible, some parts have been, some parts are to come, but no part is. The now is not a part. For the part measures and it is necessary that the whole is composed from the parts. But time is not thought to be composed out of nows.   (218ᵃ3–8)

There are two obvious ways in which one might respond to these puzzles. One response would be to claim that time is something that exists only in some atemporal sense. This would be to challenge the assumption that in order to exist, time must exist *now*. An alternative response is to claim that the present, or now, can be a part of time (either by arguing that it is not, after all, instantaneous, or by arguing that, though instantaneous, it can nevertheless be a part). Aristotle, I think, would reject both of these responses. It will help us to understand the force of these puzzles if we can explain why.

CAN WE SOLVE THE PUZZLES BY INTRODUCING SOME ATEMPORAL SENSE OF 'EXISTS'?

It is sometimes claimed that these puzzles rest upon an illusion of language. In Greek, as in English, tense is built into verbs. Because of this, it is claimed, we tend to confuse 'is' in the sense of *is a part of reality* with 'is' in the sense *is now*. There is no analogous tendency to think that if something is, it (or a part of it) must be here: a thing's relation to *here* is not built into the verbs used in speaking of it, in the way that the thing's relation to *now* is. But why should we find it any more puzzling that time can be, though no part of it is now, than that Australia can be, though no part of it is here? If Aristotle's thoughts were running along these lines, we would expect him to introduce an atemporal notion of being, a notion according to which it makes sense to say that something is but is not now. His solution would then be that it is in this atemporal sense that time is something that *is*.[3]

There is a passage later in his account in which he might seem to be introducing just such an atemporal notion of *being*. In this passage, he

---

[3] Richard Sorabji suggests a solution of this kind (without attributing it to Aristotle) in his (1983: 12–13). F. D. Miller (1974: 136) claims that Aristotle 'seems to be groping towards such a solution to the puzzle in his discussion of being in time in *Physics* IV, 12'.

claims that there are things that are but are not in time.[4] To be in time is to be surrounded by time. Something that lasts forever is not in time, since it is not surrounded by time (that is, there is no time either before or after it) (221^b3–7). It is easy to see how this passage might be thought to show that Aristotle has a notion of atemporal existence. If *not being in time* implies *not being now*, then he is claiming in this passage that things that are not surrounded by time can exist without ever being now. Since time itself, considered as a whole, is not surrounded by time, this suggests that time too can exist even if it is never true to say that it is *now*. However, as I shall argue in a later chapter, to attribute this solution to Aristotle is to misunderstand his views on being in time. When he denies that everlasting things are in time, he is not claiming that such things exist without ever being now.[5]

In any case, even if he did recognize a kind of atemporal existence, appealing to it would not solve these initial puzzles. The first puzzle is about the being not just of 'infinite time' but also of any time that 'is on any given occasion taken' (218^a1–2).[6] Whatever we say about time as a whole, there is reason to think that the finite parts of time exist temporally. We are, after all, quite happy to say that a certain year is past or that another is yet to come. Moreover, these finite parts of time

---

[4] *Physics* IV.12.221^{a}13–222^{a}9. Miller suggests that Aristotle could solve the puzzles by drawing upon his claims, in this later passage, that things that are not (but that have been or will be) are in time. Homer, for instance, is in time because he is surrounded by time. From this, Miller claims, it would be easy to arrive at the following view: to say *A existed* is just to say 'A is completely contained by the portion of time that lies before now'; to say *A will exist (in the future)* is to say that 'A is completely contained by time in the direction of the future'; to say that *A exists (in the present)* is to say that 'A is completely contained by two portions of time, one that lies before now and one that lies after now'. Miller complains that Aristotle fails to take advantage of the 'obvious solution' to his initial puzzles that is offered by this passage. Surely, he says, Aristotle need only say that to be is to be surrounded by time (Miller 1974: 139–41). But in fact, this is hopeless as a response to our initial puzzles. We cannot answer these puzzles by claiming that to be is to be surrounded by time, for the point of the puzzles was to raise doubts about whether there could be any time to do the surrounding.

[5] See below Ch. 9.

[6] For this point I am indebted to Michael Inwood's interesting discussion (1991: 156–7). Inwood claims that for temporal entities 'the tenseless use of "exist" seems to presuppose the tensed use of "exist" '. In other words, such entities are (tenselessly) only if there is some time at which it is true to say that they are now. He argues that the parts of time are temporal. (They are surrounded by time, and moreover, we use tensed discourse in speaking about them: 'The year 1066 was disastrous for England', etc.) So, if none of them is now, then none of them is (tenselessly). But in that case, time cannot be (tenselessly), since none of its parts is (tenselessly).

are 'surrounded by time', so they are 'in time' on Aristotle's view. We can generate a version of Aristotle's puzzle without mentioning infinite time at all. We can ask, for instance, about the current year. How can it be something that is, since part of it is past, part of it is future, but no part of it *is*? We cannot solve *this* version of the puzzle by invoking the notion of atemporal existence.

CAN WE SOLVE THE PUZZLES BY CLAIMING THAT THE NOW IS A PART OF TIME?

In setting out these puzzles, Aristotle assumes that the present, or 'now' as he calls it, is indivisible. Later in his account, he allows that there is a loose sense in which we can say that something is now, when we mean that it is close at hand. For example, we say 'he will come now' when we mean that he will come today and 'he has come now' when we mean that he has come today (222ª21 ff.). But strictly speaking, he maintains, the now is instantaneous.

This claim that there is something that is primarily or 'strictly speaking' now follows naturally, I think, from Aristotle's views about the difference between the past and the future. He holds that the past and present are necessary in a way that the future is not.[7] This suggests that there must be some definite division between the past and present on the one hand and the future on the other. Whether an event counts as past, present, or future cannot just depend on conversational context. It is fine to *say* 'he will come now', when one means that he will come today. But it matters that, in a stricter sense, his coming is still in the future. If it is in the future, it might still be prevented. It is not necessary, as it would be if it were genuinely present or past.[8]

---

[7] See *De Interpretatione* 9. I do not mean to imply that Aristotle thinks *everything* about the future is contingent. He holds, for instance, that it is necessarily true that the heavenly bodies will continue with their circular motions forever (see *Generation and Corruption* II.11). The difference between the future on the one hand, and the past and present on the other, is that some aspects of the future are yet to be determined, whereas everything about the past and the present is now unalterable.

[8] There is no similar temptation to think that, in addition to the vague and everyday senses in which we use the word 'here' ('Come over here', 'The weather is good here', etc.), there must be some *primary* sense of 'here'. As Owen explains, this is because we do not think that there is any such ontological difference between being to the left and being

This explains why it is natural for Aristotle to suppose that there must be some definite and non-context-relative *now* between the past and the future.[9] But why does he think that this now must be instantaneous? He defends this view later in the *Physics*.[10] The limit of the past, he argues, must be one and the same as the limit of the future. Because of this, there must be one indivisible now between the past and the future. His arguments for this are all strangely unconvincing. They assume that if there is an extended present, there must also be some other, indivisible limit of both the past and the future. He claims, for instance, that if the now is divisible, 'there will be a part of the now which has been and a part of the now which is to come and it will not always be the same part that has been or is to come' (234[a]16–18). He is assuming that within the extended now, there will, at each moment, be a different point that divides the past from the future. At any moment, the part of the now that is before this point will be past and the part of the now that is after this point will be future. But this assumption that there must be an indivisible moment that limits both the past and the future is just what someone who believes that there is an extended present means to deny.[11]

to the right: 'what *can* be counted on any occasion as past *is* then irretrievably past: it is not up to the speaker to retrieve it by deciding, within certain semantic conventions, what he will then count as past and hence as present', whereas 'what is counted as lying to the left for one purpose can on the same occasion be included in the central ground for another purpose' (Owen 1976: 305).

[9] However, it should be noted that there is another strand of Aristotle's thought that is in tension with this supposition. He holds that the now is a kind of division in a continuum. But, as I explained in the Introduction, he thinks that for a division of this sort to exist, it must be marked out in some way. Indeed, as we shall see later, his view is that we create nows (and the time they divide) by *counting* them. This raises a problem. He would not, I think, want to say that whether any given event is past (and hence necessary) depends on our counting. But he never explains how he can avoid this conclusion. He never discusses how his view that divisions in time depend on our counting can be reconciled with his view about the significance of the particular division that forms the boundary between the past and the future. This is, in fact, part of a more general puzzle about Aristotle's discussion of time in the *Physics*. It is a surprising feature of this discussion that it makes no mention of the view (defended in *De Interpretatione* 9) that whatever is past or present is necessary, whereas some events in the future are yet to be determined.

[10] *Physics* VI.3.

[11] The other arguments he gives face similar problems. He claims that if the now is divisible, 'there will be a part of the past in the future and a part of the future in the past' (234[a]12–13). That is, if the now is divisible, some point, N, in the now will mark off the future from the past. There will, then, be two limits of the past: the point N and the beginning of the now. The period of time that is after the beginning of the now but

Even if we accept that the now is instantaneous, we might wonder whether its existence could nevertheless provide the foundation for the existence of time. Aristotle's reason for thinking that it could not is that an instantaneous now is not a part of time. For something to count as a *part*, it must be the sort of thing with which we could measure a whole (218ᵃ6–7), but the now, being indivisible, cannot be a unit with which we measure time. Moreover, a whole is composed of its parts, but, as Aristotle has argued elsewhere, something continuous, like time, cannot be composed entirely of indivisibles.[12]

However, this simply invites a further question. Granted that an indivisible cannot be a *part* of something continuous, what justifies the assumption that for time to be, a part of it would have to be? Why is it not possible for a continuous thing, like time, to exist in virtue of the existence of an indivisible point in it?

Aristotle does not discuss this question, but he could, I think, respond to it by drawing upon the views about continuity and indivisibility that I outlined in the Introduction.[13] On his view, an indivisible must always be a boundary of, or potential division in, some extended thing. It is, in other words, a dependent kind of entity. Because of this, if an indivisible is to exist, there must be something for it to bound or divide. This suggests that the now's existence must depend on that of time, rather than vice versa.

ARISTOTLE'S DEFINITION OF TIME AND THE PUZZLES ABOUT WHETHER TIME IS

I have discussed both the proposal that the puzzles should be solved by introducing an atemporal sense of 'exists' and also the proposal that the existence of the now is by itself enough to provide a foundation for

---

before N will be both future (because it is after the beginning of the now, which is the limit of the past) and past (because it is after N, which is another limit of the past and the future). (I am indebted here to Hasper 2003: ch. 3, pp. 107–8.) Also, if the now is divisible, 'the now will be a now not in its own right but in virtue of something else' (234ᵃ14–15) (since the now will be a now in virtue of spanning the period of time that contains the point of division between the past and the future).

[12] *Physics* VI.1.231ᵃ21–ᵇ18.
[13] See above, pp. 9–13.

the existence of time. Aristotle would not have accepted either of these two solutions. It remains, then, to consider whether some other solution is implicit in the account of time that he goes on to give. He is going to define time as something that is essentially dependent on change. His view is that for time to be, there must be changes and these changes must, in some sense to be explained, be countable. Is this enough to solve his initial puzzles about time? Can we claim that, although there is a sense in which all there is of time is the now, time can nevertheless exist in virtue of its relation to change? The idea would be to appeal to the fact that the now is not merely a potential division in time, but also a potential division in changes. If there are these changes (and if we can order them in a certain way by counting nows), perhaps that is all that is needed for there to be time.

Much more explanation is needed if this suggestion is to be at all clear. To understand it properly, one would need to understand the whole of Aristotle's account of time—the project of the book, rather than of this chapter. But even at this early stage, there is something that can usefully be said. The suggestion is that time *is* in virtue of the fact that changes are (together with the fact that they are 'countable', a qualification I shall explain later in the book). To defend this sugges-tion, it is necessary to explain how the claim that the being of time depends on the being of changes gets us any further forward. The difficulty is that it seems as if the puzzle about the parts of time can simply be extended to changes. Of any change that is going on, part has been, part is to come, and all that there *is* is an indivisible instant. But an indivisible instant is not a part of the change and hence (so the argument would go) cannot be the basis for the existence of the change. The initial puzzles could even be taken to show that nothing more than an instantaneous slice of anything ever exists. Anything, the claim would be, can be divided into temporal parts, and once we think of something as divided in this way it becomes apparent that it is composed entirely of a past part that no longer is and a future part that is yet to be.

If the puzzles could be extended in this way, then an appeal to the fact that time depends upon change would provide no solution to them. It is interesting that Aristotle never does extend the puzzles to raise doubts

about the being either of changes or of changing things.[14] The reason
for this, I think, is that he takes it for granted first, that for a change to be
is for a changing thing to be changing and, second, that changing things
do not have temporal parts.

I gave an outline of Aristotle's account of change in the Introduction.[15] We saw there that a thing is changing in virtue of the fact that it
has a potential to be otherwise and this potential is, in a certain
particular sense, actual. For example, I am travelling to the moon just
in case (i) I have a potential to be on the moon, (ii) this potential is
actual (it is not just lying dormant) and (iii) it is actual only in so far as it
is potential (I have not yet reached the moon). To ask whether a change
is is to ask whether the change *is going on*. A change will be going on if
and only if there is some changing thing that has a potentiality that is, in
the relevant sense, actual.[16] On Aristotle's view, the changing thing does
not itself have temporal parts.[17] There is no reason, then, to deny that
the changing thing is something that is. *It* is not made up of parts that
are past and parts that are future. Hence the change too is something
that is, for its being depends, in the way I have described, on the being

[14] Moreover, none of the Greek commentators suggests that the puzzles should be
extended in this way. Simplicius (*In Phys.* 696), drawing on Aristotle's discussion of the
infinite, gives examples of things that exist at a time because either some or all of their
parts exist then. Things that exist when all of their parts exist are 'a line, a surface and a
body'. Things that exist because a part of them exists are 'things that have their being in
becoming, as in a contest or a change'. For Simplicius, as for Aristotle, changes and
persisting things are *unlike* time in this respect. When the discussion is about things in
time rather than time itself, there is never any suggestion that all that exists is an
instantaneous slice.

[15] See above, pp. 5–9.

[16] This argument is, of course, only as convincing as Aristotle's account of change. I
raise some difficulties for this account (and in particular for the view that anything that
has a potential that is in the relevant sense actual will be changing) in the Introduction, n.
19

[17] In explaining, for example, how a man can be first unmusical and then musical, he
says, not that a temporal part of the man is unmusical and another temporal part of him
is musical, but rather that one and the same underlying thing, the man, persists through
the change, first having the accidental property of unmusicality (and having the potential
to be musical) and then having the accidental property of musicality (*Physics* I.7–8). (In
Physics VI.4.234^{b}10–20, in the course of an argument that anything that changes must
be divisible, he does claim that a subject that is changing from white to grey must have a
part that is white and a part that is grey, but this is a claim about spatial, not temporal
parts.)

of the changing thing. For the change to be is just for the changing thing to have a potential that is, in the relevant sense, actual.[18]

THE THIRD PUZZLE: IS THE NOW ALWAYS DIFFERENT OR ALWAYS THE SAME?

The first two puzzles were about time and its relation to the now. The third puzzle concerns the now itself. Aristotle argues that we get into difficulties if we say either that the now is always different or that it is always the same.

It cannot be the case that each instant, or 'now', is different. If it were, we should be able to ask when the *present* instant has first ceased to exist.[19] But, Aristotle argues, there is no satisfactory answer to this question. For example, let the current time be five o'clock. When will the instant that is now first have ceased to exist? It cannot have ceased to exist at five o'clock, for that is when it exists. But it also cannot have ceased to exist at the very next instant after five o'clock. This is because there *is* no very next instant after five o'clock (since no two instants are next to each other).[20] The only other alternative seems to be that it has

---

[18] The argument I have given assumes that it is possible for something to be changing now. It is possible, that is, to be changing at the instant that is the boundary between the past and the future. Something is changing now just in case it now has a potential that is actual in the relevant sense. Commentators have sometimes claimed that an argument of Aristotle's at *Physics* VI.3. 234ᵃ24–31 rules out the possibility of changing at a now. Aristotle argues there that nothing *kineitai en* a now. How to translate this is controversial. '*Kineitai*' can mean either 'is changing' or 'changes' and '*en*' can mean either 'at' or 'in'. Owen claims that the translation should be 'is changing at' and that Aristotle is saying that nothing can be changing at a now (Owen 1976: 296–301). But this is unconvincing as an interpretation of his argument in these lines. The argument has the form of a *reductio*. If it were possible for a changing thing, X, to change in a now, then (since changes can be quicker or slower) it would have to be possible for another changing thing, Y, to perform the same change more quickly (i.e. in less time than the now). But that is not possible, since the now is indivisible. The claim, then, is about whether it is possible to *perform a change in* a now, not about whether it is possible to *be changing at* a now.

[19] The question Aristotle asks is 'when has it ceased to exist?', not 'when has it *first* ceased to exist?'. However, the argument he gives shows that he means 'when has it first ceased to exist?'. That is why if there is a period of time between when the now exists and when it has ceased to exist, it follows that the now must exist during that period.

[20] This claim presupposes Aristotle's view that time is continuous. Between any two instants, there will always be a divisible period of time.

first ceased to exist at some later instant that is not next to five o'clock. But in that case, it will have existed for a period of time: it will have remained in existence throughout all the intervening instants. As Aristotle says:

> It cannot have ceased to be in itself, because of its existing then, and to have ceased to be in another now is impossible for the earlier now. For let us say that it is impossible for nows to be next to each other, as it is for a point to a point. So if it has not perished in the next, but in another, it will exist together with the infinitely many in-between nows. But this is impossible. (218ª16–21)[21]

That is why the now cannot be always different. Could it, instead, be always the same? Aristotle gives two reasons why it could not. First, he says, any finite time period must have two boundaries: 'nothing that is divisible and limited has only one boundary, whether it is continuous in one direction or in more than one' (218ª22–4).[22] But if the now were always the same, then finite parts of time would not have two different boundaries.

The other reason why the now cannot always be the same is that, if it were, then things that happened a thousand years ago would be simultaneous with things that were happening today (since they would all be at the same now):

> Further, if to be together in time and neither before nor after is to be at one and the same now, and if earlier and later [nows] are at this very now, then events of a thousand years ago will be simultaneous with events of today and nothing will be either before or after anything else. (218ª25–30)

How might Aristotle answer these puzzles about the sameness and difference of the now? He does have more to say about the now later in his account. As we shall see, he claims that the now is in a way always the same, but also in a way always different. But these later remarks do not, I think, provide us with a satisfying solution. The claim that the now remains always the same while being always different simply gives

---

[21] The reason for Aristotle's use of the perfect in this passage (*has ceased*, rather than *is ceasing*) is that indivisible things do not go through a *process* of ceasing to exist. There is, then, no time at which an indivisible thing is (in the process of) ceasing to exist.

[22] That is, whether it is two-dimensional or three-dimensional.

rise to a new puzzle. Instead of being a puzzle about when the now has first *perished*, it is a puzzle about when the now has first *become different.*[23]

We can arrive at a better solution by drawing on Aristotle's views about continuity. As I explained in the Introduction, Aristotle thinks that indivisibles only exist in a continuum in so far as they are marked out in some way. A line does not contain infinitely many points, but it is infinitely divisible. I can create a point (that is, a potential division) anywhere on it. When Aristotle says that between any two points on a line, there is always another, what he means, strictly speaking, is that between any two points, another point could always have been marked. Similarly time, though it is not composed of infinitely many nows, is infinitely divisible: between any two nows, another now could always have been marked.[24]

With this in mind, it is possible to defend the view that the now is always different. The argument that made this view seem impossible assumed the existence of a densely ordered series of nows. Suppose instead that there is a now only when a now is marked out in some way.[25] In that case, there is an answer to the question: when has the now that was at five o'clock first ceased to exist? It has first ceased to exist *in the time between five o'clock and the first actual now that is marked out after five o'clock*. If someone demands a more exact answer, asking *when*

[23] When has the now first become different from the way it was at five o'clock? It cannot already have become different at five o'clock. It cannot have become different at the next instant after five o'clock (since there is no such instant). But if there is a period of time between five o'clock and when the now has first become different from how it was at five o'clock, then the now cannot be different during that period of time (which contradicts the claim that it is always different).

[24] I explain this account of continuity more fully in the Introduction. As I say there, a potential division in a line is a point at which the line could actually be cut into two physically separate parts. Aristotle says that the now is, analogously, a potential division in time, though time cannot actually be divided into two separate parts. See above pp. 9–13.

[25] For the purposes of *this* argument, it is not necessary to settle what exactly has to be true for a now to be 'marked out' (though obviously, if the solution I propose is to work, *the now's having first ceased to exist* cannot itself be an event that marks out a now). I argue, in Chs. 5 and 7, that *we* mark nows by counting the limits of, and potential divisions in, changes. As I explain in Chapter 10, this has important consequences for the relation between time and ensouled beings (see pp. 169–72).

during this time period the five o'clock now first has ceased to exist, we can reply that, since no now has been marked out during this time, there is no more exact answer to be given.[26]

It is interesting to compare this to a solution that naturally suggests itself to the modern reader. A natural modern response is to deny that there is any instant at which the five o'clock now has first ceased to exist; it has ceased to exist at *any* subsequent now.[27] The solution I have attributed to Aristotle has much in common with this modern response. His point is that however soon after five o'clock we were to mark out a now, the five o'clock now would already have perished in the period of time before then. But the Aristotelian solution, unlike its modern counterpart, can *explain* why there is no instant at which the five o'clock now has first ceased to exist: the now has ceased to exist in a period of time in which no instant has been marked out.

If I am right, the Aristotelian solution to this puzzle depends on the view that nows, like other indivisibles, only exist if they are in some way marked out from a continuum. This brings out something important about the relation between this third puzzle and the earlier two. The assumption that the now is an essentially dependent entity, an assumption I have appealed to in solving this third puzzle, was precisely what made the initial two puzzles seem insoluble.

Our problem was this. On the one hand, none of time *is* except the now. This suggests that time only exists in virtue of the existence of the now. But on the other hand, for the now to exist, it must be a division or boundary of some independently existing continuum. This continuum cannot be *time*, since time itself is dependent on the now.[28] It follows that there must be some *other* continuum, prior to time, on which the now depends for its existence. I have already hinted that this other

---

[26] Of course, that is not to say that *having first ceased to exist* is something that happens over a period of time. It is merely to say that there is no more exact specification of when it happens, than that it happens during a certain period.

[27] This is, indeed, how Sorabji suggests that Aristotle would solve the puzzle (1983: 10–12).

[28] This is not to deny that the now is a boundary between the past and the future. It is just to deny that the past and the future form a continuum that exists independently of the now.

continuum is change.[29] The now is a potential division in all the changes that are going on at it. This is a claim that I shall examine at greater length in the following chapters. As we shall see, the idea that time and the now both depend for their existence on changes plays a central role in Aristotle's account.

---

[29] See above, pp. 23–6.

2

Time is Not Change but Something of Change

Aristotle's positive account starts out from the assumption that time is, as he puts it, 'something of change'.[1] The nature of time is constituted by its relation to change and an account of time must explain what this relation is. But he does not simply state this at the outset. Instead, he makes some remarks that are designed to show that it is a reasonable thing to assume.

The remarks are of two types. First, he examines his predecessors' accounts of time. He focuses particularly on the view that time is a kind of change.[2] Though he argues that this view is mistaken, he thinks its proponents are onto something right. They have seen that there is a close relationship between time and change. Second, he looks at various common beliefs about time and change. We tend to think that there is no time without change and there is no change without time. The assumption that time is 'something of change' provides some justification for these ordinary beliefs.

To appeal in this way to the views of his predecessors and to our ordinary assumptions is standard Aristotelian practice. There is, he thinks, reason to believe that there will be *some* truth in such views. As he says in the *Metaphysics*,

---

[1] 'Something of change' is awkward English. I am using it to express what in French would be expressed by 'quelque chose du changement'. In English it would be more natural to say 'some aspect of change' but I want to avoid this translation because it suggests that time is a *property* of change. Aristotle's point is that the definition of time (the account of what time is) will make essential reference to change.

[2] He also briefly mentions (and dismisses) another view. He says that some people thought that the sphere of the universe was time, on the grounds that everything is in the sphere of the universe and everything is in time. He brushes this view aside with the remark that it is too simple-minded to be worth discussing (218^b5–9).

No one is able to hit on the truth adequately, though no one misses it completely. But each says something right about the nature of things, and though each by himself contributes little or nothing to the truth, all together contribute quite a lot.[3]

By criticizing his predecessors, Aristotle aims to extract from their views a kernel of truth. Though they were all mistaken, they did not miss the truth completely. They had the insight that time must be 'something of change'. This insight, he goes on to show, is also behind our everyday assumptions about whether or not time has passed.

THE VIEW THAT TIME IS A KIND OF CHANGE

The view that time is a kind of change may have been held by members of the Academy. One of the academic *Definitions* describes time as 'the motion of the sun'[4] and Plato himself is prepared to say, in the *Timaeus*, that time is 'the wandering of the heavenly bodies' (39d).[5] Aristotle first criticizes the view that time is a certain particular change: the rotation of the universe (218ª33–ᵇ5). He then goes on to argue more generally that time cannot be any kind of change.

In attacking the view that time is the movement of the universe, he gives one argument that is of particular interest.[6] The argument reveals a central assumption that lies behind his account: the assumption that there can only be one time series. Time, he says, cannot be the movement of the universe. If it were, then the fact that there is just one time series would depend on the fact that there is only one universe (that is,

---

[3] *Metaphysics* II.1 993ª31–ᵇ4.

[4] Plato *Definitions*, 411b. The *Definitions*, ascribed to Plato, is a collection of definitions, generally thought to have been coined by members of the Academy. See D. S. Hutchinson in Cooper (1997: 1677–8).

[5] However, it is, I think, unlikely that this was Plato's considered view. When he describes time as the 'wandering of the heavenly bodies' in the *Timaeus*, he seems to be speaking loosely. When he is being more careful, he says only that the heavenly bodies were created so that they could, with their movements, 'mark off and preserve the numbers of time' (38c).

[6] The other argument he gives is that time cannot be a kind of revolution (as the movement of the universe would be: 218ᵇ1–3). His reason is that a part of time is a time, whereas a part of a revolution is not a revolution. The point, presumably, is that a repeated circular movement does not have the right kind of structure to be time. Time does not come divided into natural units as a movement of this kind does.

only one set of heavens).[7] Two moving universes would give us two time series: 'if the heavens were more, time would equally be the change of each of them, so that there would be many times together (*hama*)' (218^b3–5).[8]

What makes this argument particularly interesting is that Aristotle himself thinks that there can only be one universe.[9] This raises a prima facie puzzle. If he thinks that there is necessarily only one universe, then why is he asking what *would* be the case if there were several of them? One would expect him to think that, whatever other faults it has, the view that time is the movement of the universe does at least capture the uniqueness of time: just as there can only be one universe, so also there can only be one time series.

To understand what he is saying here, one has to appreciate that there are different senses in which something might be necessarily unique. His point is that time is by its very nature unique, in a way that the universe is not. Though there is necessarily only one universe, this is not something that is true *because of what it is to be a universe*. Rather, it is something that follows from other necessary facts about the way things are.[10]

When he argues, in the *De Caelo*, that there can only be one universe, or heaven, he says that since the heaven is a particular,

there will be a difference between *being this heaven* and *being a heaven in general*. Therefore, *this heaven* and *a heaven in general* will be different; the one is form

---

[7] In our passage, Aristotle refers to the universe both as 'the whole', *to holon* (218^a33) and as 'the heavens' *hoi ouranoi* (218^b4).

[8] It is a little misleading to say, as Aristotle does here, that there would be 'many times together' (especially as *hama*, the word I translate as 'together' here, also means 'simultaneous'). In fact, on this view, if there were several universes, there would be several *temporally unrelated* time series. There would be no overarching time within which the movements of the different universes were related to one another, so the different times would not be *together*.

[9] He defends this claim in *De Caelo* I.9. By 'the universe' here (and in our passage of the *Physics*) he means *the cosmos*, rather than *the entirety of everything physical*. As we shall see, he has an argument that everything physical is contained in the universe (*De Caelo* I.9. 278^b21–279^a11), but this is something that has to be established by argument. It is not simply true by definition.

[10] In this argument, I rely on a distinction between necessary truths about a thing that follow from its essence and other necessary truths about the thing. This distinction will become important again in my discussion of time and the soul in Ch. 10. It is a distinction that is drawn and usefully explained by Kit Fine (1994). I am not suggesting that Aristotle had a fully developed account of this distinction. My claim is only that a distinction of this kind is presupposed by his argument here.

and shape, the other is form in combination with matter; and in the case of things that have a shape or form, there either are or there can be many particulars. (278ᵃ12–16)

'Heaven' and 'universe' are universals and, as such, are things of which there can in theory be more than one instance. However, there cannot in fact be a plurality of universes. This is because our universe contains all the matter there is: there is no matter left for any other universes (278ᵃ26–8). The claim that there is no matter outside this universe follows from Aristotle's view that there are no natural places outside this universe. He argues that if there had been any matter elsewhere, it would already have moved back to its natural place in this universe.[11] The reason why there cannot be more than one universe is, then, that no other universe could contain any matter.

We can now understand why he says that time cannot be the movement of the universe. The universe, unlike time, is the *sort of thing* of which there could be two. If time were the movement of the universe, it would still be necessarily true that there was only one time series (since there is, necessarily, only one universe), but this would not be a necessity that followed *simply from the nature of time*. Thus, the account of time as the movement of the universe fails to capture the fact that time is something that is by its very nature unique.[12]

Aristotle goes on to give two arguments, of a more general nature, against the view that time is a kind of movement or change. The first is that a movement or change is only in the changing thing, whereas time is equally everywhere and in everything (218ᵇ10–13). The second is that change is faster and slower whereas time is not (218ᵇ13–18).

In the first of these arguments, Aristotle points out two related ways in which changes differ from time. A change, he claims, is always localized: it occurs at some place rather than another. Moreover, every change is associated with some thing: it is 'in the changing thing'. Time

---

[11] *De Caelo* I.9. 278ᵇ21–279ᵃ11.

[12] It might seem that there is still a further possibility: could time be a change in *whatever exists*? That is, can we say: if there is just one universe, time is the change in it; if there were two universes, time would be the change in *both* of these, and so on? Aristotle's answer, I think, would be that a collection of several universes need not form a whole, and that unless something is in some sense a whole, it is not the right kind of entity to be the subject of a change. We cannot, then, just assume that *everything that exists* will have the right kind of unity to be the subject of a single change.

is neither. It is (and is necessarily) the same everywhere, and it is just as much with one thing as it is with another.

Since time is thought particularly to be movement and a kind of change, this must be examined. The movement and change of each thing is only in the changing thing itself or wherever the moving or changing thing itself happens to be. But time is similarly both everywhere and with everything.   (218^{b}9–13)

This argument depends on a certain assumption about the universality of time. There is one time that is the time of everything, but there is no one change that is the change of everything. Even if it made sense to think of all changes as partaking in some one super-change, this super-change could not be time. For such a super-change would not be by its very nature all-encompassing, in the way in which (Aristotle thinks) time is.

The assumption that time is in some sense universal—that there is one time for many changes—will be important in Aristotle's positive account of time, but at this stage, it is not clear in exactly what sense it is true that time is 'similarly both everywhere and with everything'. This claim could be taken in a very strong sense, to mean both that time is just as much in one place as another and that it is related to each thing in just the same way as it is related to every other thing. But the account Aristotle goes on to give would be at odds with this very strong reading. He does not think that time stands in exactly the same relationship to everything that exists. He argues, for instance, that certain things (things last forever) are not in time.[13] However, the claim that time is 'similarly both everywhere and with everything' need not be taken in this strong sense. The word 'similarly' (*homoiōs*) need not signify that everything is related to time *in the same way*. Aristotle's claim is, I think, simply that time is *both* everywhere and with everything. To say that time is 'with everything' is to say that each thing is at some point in one and the same time series.[14]

As we shall see, this emphasis on the universality of time gives rise to a problem Aristotle will face when he comes to give his own positive account. He is going to argue that time is something that is defined, at least in part, by its relation to change. One important task will be to

[13] I discuss this argument in Ch. 9 below.
[14] As we shall see later, when he says that there are certain things that are not in time, he does not mean to deny that these things exist at a time.

explain how it is possible, given time's close relation to change, for there to be one and the same time series, though there are many different changes. How, that is, can there be one time series that is 'with everything'?

Aristotle's second general argument against the view that time is a kind of change is that changes can go faster and slower, whereas time cannot:

> Change is faster and slower. But time is not. For the slow and the fast are defined by time, fast being the thing moving much in little time, slow being the thing moving little in much. But time is not defined by time, not by its being so much nor by its being of such a sort. It is clear, then, that time is not change.   (218^b13-18)

Changes are the sort of things that can be faster or slower.[15] What it is for something to be faster or slower is for it to change a greater or smaller amount in a certain amount of time. It follows that it must make sense to say of any change, that a certain amount of it passed in a certain amount of time. But, Aristotle thinks, it does not make sense to say this of time itself: time is not defined by time.

For us, part of the interest of this argument lies in its striking resemblance to certain attempts by modern philosophers to show that time cannot be something that passes. These philosophers have argued that it is misleading to say that time passes, since if it were to pass it would have to do so at a certain rate. A version of this argument is presented by Huw Price:

> If it made sense to say that time flows then it would make sense to ask how fast it flows, which doesn't seem to be a sensible question. Some people reply that time flows at one second per second, but even if we could live with the lack of other possibilities, this answer misses the more basic aspect of the objection. A rate of seconds per second is not a rate at all in physical terms. It is a dimensionless quantity, rather than a rate of any sort.   (Price 1996: 13)

The objection that time might pass at a rate of a second per second is just the kind of objection that Aristotle is anticipating and rejecting

---

[15] This is an assumption Aristotle also makes elsewhere. For instance, it is a crucial part of his argument that pleasure cannot be a process, in the *Nicomachean Ethics* (X.3.1173^{a}31 ff.). Also, later in the account of time, Aristotle argues that all changes must be in time on the grounds that they can all be fast or slow (*Physics* IV.14.222^{b}30–223^{a}15).

when he says that time is not defined by time.[16] The similarity between Aristotle's argument and Price's argument suggests a question. Price is arguing against the view that time flows. Does Aristotle's argument have a similar target? That is, in refuting the claim that time is a kind of change, does he take himself to have shown that time is not the kind of thing that can be said to *pass*?

At this stage of the account it is too early to say. But we can at least note that Aristotle shows himself here to be aware of one of the main arguments that modern philosophers have brought against the view that time passes. Later in his account, he is going to compare the now to a moving thing. Whether or not, in doing so, he is embracing the view that time passes is a matter for debate. At the very least, his initial arguments against the view that time is a kind of change raise an important question about his own account. In what sense can the now be like a moving thing, given that the now is not the sort of thing that can be said to go fast or slow? This is a question to which I return in Chapter 8.

TIME AS 'SOMETHING OF CHANGE': THE APPEAL TO ORDINARY JUDGEMENTS

Having dismissed his predecessors' view that time is a kind of change, Aristotle goes on to bring out the truth that lies behind this view. Time is not change, but is 'something of change'. At any rate, this is an appropriate assumption with which to start out an inquiry into time:

It is clear that time is not change and that it is not without change. So it remains, since we are inquiring into what time is, to start out from this and ask what it is of change. (219ᵃ1–3)

His argument that this is the assumption with which to start invokes our ordinary judgements about whether or not time has passed. He draws attention to the fact that certain beliefs about the relation between time and change are presupposed in our ordinary thinking about time. When we think there has been no change, we think that no time has passed.

---

[16] For an interesting modern defence of the claim that a second per second is a genuine rate, see Maudlin (2002: 239–41).

We assume, that is, that there can be no time without change. On the other hand, if we think that there has been any change, then we think that time must have passed, since we take it for granted that there can be no change without time.

Aristotle obviously thinks that his claim that time is 'not without change' is supported by these facts about our ordinary judgements. But why, exactly, does he think this? What is the point of appealing to these ordinary judgements at the start of his account of time? The answer is that he is taking for granted a certain methodological principle: the fact that something is assumed in our ordinary judgements gives us a prima facie reason to believe it. Any inquiry needs to start out from some assumptions. A question then arises about what our initial assumptions should be. Aristotle's view is that when certain beliefs can be shown to lie behind our ordinary judgements, it is reasonable to start out by taking these beliefs to be true.[17]

This method is familiar from elsewhere in his work. In his inquiry into place, for instance, he says that it is best to proceed in such a way that the difficulties about place are solved and the things thought to be true of it (*ta dokounta huparchein*) are shown really to be true of it (*Physics* IV.4.211ᵃ7–11). He begins his account of time by raising certain puzzles and by showing that one of the things commonly said about time—that it is a kind of change—cannot be right. He now lays out certain other assumptions that we tend to make about time: that there is time *when* there is change and *only when* there is change. Unless there is some argument for thinking that these assumptions too are mistaken, it is reasonable to take them as the basis for an inquiry into the nature of time.

---

[17] I have spoken of beliefs that 'lie behind' or are 'presupposed by' the judgements we make. But what is it for a belief to be 'presupposed by' the judgements we make? Aristotle is not claiming that we all explicitly believe that there is no time without change or change without time. His claim is only that these beliefs would explain and justify the particular judgements we make about whether or not time has passed. Compare his discussion of the voluntary in the *Nicomachean Ethics*. He claims there that 'whatever has its principle in us is itself in our power and voluntary' (*Nicomachean Ethics* III, 5, 1113ᵇ20–1). As evidence for this, he describes the way that we assign punishment and praise (1113ᵇ21–30). When he cites this as evidence, he is not saying that we all have the explicit belief that the acts that originate from moving principles in us are the ones that are voluntary. He is saying, rather, that this is a belief which explains and justifies our judgements when we assign praise and blame.

That is Aristotle's strategy in this passage. Let us look in more detail at the claims he makes about our ordinary judgements. He claims, first, that we ordinarily assume that there is no time without change (218^{b}29–31). When we do not think that there has been change, we assume that no time has passed. If nothing in our mind alters (or we don't notice it altering), it seems to us that there has been no time (218^{b}21–3). Those who sleep dreamlessly in the cave with the Sardinian heroes don't know, when they wake up, that any time has passed because there is no way for them to tell the difference between the now at which they fell asleep and the now at which they woke up: 'They join the earlier now to the later now and make them one' (218^{b}25–6). In order to differentiate between the two nows, they would have to know that something had changed.

These observations, he seems to think, by themselves provide grounds for assuming that time is something related to change (219^{a}2–3). But he goes on to give some additional support for making this assumption. He points out that we perceive time and change together (219^{a}3–4). Whenever we perceive a change, we conclude that time must have passed. Even if it is dark and we can't see or hear anything, so long as we are aware of a change in our soul, then we think that time has passed (219^{a}4–6). His point seems to be that not only do we assume that there is no time without change, we also assume that there is no change without time. This provides another reason for thinking that time is something closely related to change. It also, perhaps, provides some justification for a further claim. The fact that the occurrence of *any* change is enough to show that time has passed supports the assumption that time is essentially related to change in general, rather than to some *particular* change.[18]

For the purposes of Aristotle's inquiry, then, it is reasonable to assume that there is no time without change and, moreover, that there is no change without time.[19] He has already shown that time is not itself a

---

[18] This gives Aristotle some reason to define time as a number of *change* rather than as a number of *the change of the outermost heavenly sphere*.

[19] Aristotle doesn't make the latter point explicitly here. But it must surely be what we are supposed to infer from the observation that we think time has passed whenever we notice a change. Later, he gives an argument that all change is in time (*Physics* IV.14. 222^{b}30–223^{a}15).

certain kind of change. This suggests that it is, instead, something closely related to change. He concludes that:

Either time is change or it is something of change. So, since it is not change, it is necessary that it is something of change. (219ᵃ8–10)

AN ALTERNATIVE INTERPRETATION?

Aristotle's remarks in this opening section of chapter 11 are often interpreted quite differently. He is often taken to be making the assumption that the passage of time must, in principle, be detectable. On this interpretation, his argument is that we can only detect the passage of time if there is change, and hence that there can be no time without change.[20]

This interpretation has two main weaknesses. The first weakness is that there is no independent reason to think that Aristotle endorsed the premiss that the passage of time must be detectable.[21] He does not himself say, in the passage with which we are concerned, that there can be no undetectable times and there is no evidence elsewhere to suggest that he held this view. In contrast, the methodological assumption that I attribute to him fits well with his practice elsewhere.

Someone might suppose that material later in Aristotle's account could be used to supply the missing premiss. For instance, Edward Hussey (1993: 142) has suggested that a later argument, in which Aristotle defends the view that there could be no time in a world without animate beings, might be an attempt to supply such a premiss. But this cannot be right. The later argument is drawing out a conse-

---

[20] This is the interpretation suggested by Sorabji (1983: 75). Compare Edward Hussey (1993: 142): Aristotle's argument 'seems to require the extra premiss that all lapse of time is perceptible'. Compare also Shoemaker (1969: 365–6): Aristotle's argument 'seems to be that time involves change because the awareness, or realization, that an interval of time has elapsed necessarily involves the awareness of changes occurring during the interval'. See Coope (2001) for a fuller argument against this interpretation.

[21] In fact, as Richard Sorabji notes (1983: 75), this interpretation has to supply *two* unstated premisses: not only the premiss that the passage of time must be detectable but also the premiss that it is impossible to perceive time without change. In our passage, Aristotle does not actually say that it is *impossible* to perceive time without change, though one might expect him to say this explicitly if the proposed interpretation were right.

quence of Aristotle's definition of time as a number of change (223^a21–9). And this definition itself depends on the assumption that there can be no time without change, since it is that assumption that allows us to start out the inquiry by taking it for granted that time is 'something of change'.

The other main weakness in this alternative interpretation is that in the passage we are considering, Aristotle says not just that we are aware that time has passed only when we are aware that there has been some change, but also that we think that there has been a change only when we think that time has passed (218^b32–3, 219^a3–6). On my interpretation, both of these claims play the same kind of role in Aristotle's argument.[22] The first is evidence that we take it for granted that there can be no time without change. The second is evidence that we take it for granted that there can be no change without time.[23] Both claims together are grounds for the assumption that time is either a kind of change or something very closely connected to change. It is hard, on the alternative interpretation, to explain the role in the argument of the claim that we think there has been time whenever we perceive a change.[24] There is no plausible premiss about the detectability of either time or change that we could add to this second claim in order to reach a conclusion about the relation between time and change.

---

[22] There is, admittedly, one thing that is puzzling about the structure of this argument. Aristotle writes as if his remark at 218^b32–3, 'but whenever we perceive and mark off a change, then we say that there has been time', is one of the grounds for concluding that there is no time without change. This is a difficulty for *any* interpretation. The best solution, I think, is to take this remark as parenthetical.

[23] It may be objected that the claim that there can be no change without time is too obviously true to need justification. But for Aristotle, it may not have seemed so obvious. Aristotle's definition of change makes no explicit reference to time. Change is defined in terms of actuality and potentiality (*Physics* III.1.201^a9–11). Moreover, if we take the creation story in the *Timaeus* literally, as Aristotle did (*De Caelo* I.10. 280^a30–2), then Plato thought that there were disorderly movements before the creation of time (*Timaeus*, 30a, 52d).

[24] Shoemaker ignores this second claim. He presents Aristotle as holding simply that 'the awareness ... that an interval of time has elapsed necessarily involves the awareness of changes occurring during the interval' (1969: 365–6). Sorabji is more careful. He says that, for Aristotle, we notice time *when and only when* we notice change (1983: 74). But Sorabji does not remark on the fact that on his interpretation, half of this premiss seems redundant.

WHY ASSUME THAT TIME IS SOMETHING
OF CHANGE, RATHER THAN THAT CHANGE
IS SOMETHING OF TIME?

Aristotle doesn't just start out by assuming that time and change are closely related. He assumes that time is something of change—that is, that time's nature is defined partly in terms of its relation to change. But why assume that *this* is the way in which they are related? For all that has been said so far, he could equally well conclude that time is basic and that change is to be understood in terms of its relation to time.[25]

Throughout his account of time, he takes it for granted that change is somehow more basic than time. In the context of the *Physics*, this is, perhaps, only to be expected. After all, in an earlier part of the *Physics* he has given an account of change that makes no explicit reference to time (*Physics* III.1–2). This already implies that change is not something that is to be defined in terms of its relation to time.

But why is it natural for him to make this assumption that it is time that is defined in terms of change rather than vice versa? One possible answer is that changes are more closely related to particular substances than time is. A change, as we have already seen, is always a change in some *thing*. Aristotle's account of change is an account of what it is for a particular substance to change.[26] The relation between time and any particular substance is less direct. Those substances that come to be and pass away are all in time. But one and the same period of time will equally be the time in which many such substances are. Time, that is, is universal in a way in which changes and changing things are not. This provides Aristotle with some reason to think that changes are ontologically more basic than time. Particular substances have a fundamental role

[25] On my interpretation, this problem is particularly salient, since Aristotle is arguing that we should assume both that there is no time without change and that there is no change without time. But this is not a problem that is *created* by my interpretation. The alternative interpretation simply masks the problem by ignoring half of what Aristotle says.

[26] See pp. 5–9, above. He claims, at *Categories* 5.4^{a}10–^{b}19, that a distinctive feature of particular substances is that they can be subjects of change.

in his ontology. If changes are more closely related to particular substances than time is, it is natural to suppose that they are ontologically more basic than it. Given this background, it is unsurprising that his initial assumption is that time is 'something of change', not that change is 'something of time'.

PART II

TIME'S DEPENDENCE
ON CHANGE

3

Time Follows Change and Change Follows Magnitude

Aristotle's next step is to explain the way in which time is related to change: 'what it is of change' (219^{a}3). He proceeds to outline certain relations of dependency that hold, both between time and change and between change and what he calls 'magnitude':[1]

Since the changing thing changes from something to something and all magnitude is continuous, the change follows the magnitude. For through the magnitude's being continuous the change too is continuous, but through the change, the time. For the amount of time that has passed is always thought to be as much as the amount of change. Therefore,[2] the before and after is first of all in place. And there it is in position. But since the before and after is in magnitude, it is necessary that also the before and after is in change, by analogy with the things there. But the before and after is also in time, through the following always of the one upon the other of them. (219^{a}10–19)

This paragraph is of central importance for Aristotle's account, but it is particularly condensed and open to various different interpretations. How are we to understand these relations of dependency? What does Aristotle mean here by 'change' and 'magnitude'? What are these different kinds of before and after? And how can the before and after in change be in some sense prior to the before and after in time? These are just some of the questions that, as readers, we have to ask ourselves. It is a measure of the complexity of this short but suggestive passage that I shall spend the whole of Part II unpacking what Aristotle says here.

---

[1] I shall argue that by this he means spatially extended magnitude—that is, the extension of a spatially extended thing.

[2] In translating '$d\acute{e}$' here as 'therefore', I follow Owen (1976: 301, fn.15) and Ross (1936: 386).

Aristotle introduces, in this passage, the relation of *following*. Time, he says, follows change and change follows magnitude. Presumably, to say that X follows Y is to say that Y is, in some sense, prior to X. But what kind of priority does he have in mind? His emphasis in the preceding section on how we *know* that time has passed, might suggest that the priority is epistemological: we come to know about certain features of time, by knowing corresponding features of change, and we come to know these features of change by knowing corresponding features of magnitude. However, such epistemological dependence would not be asymmetric in the way that a relation of *following* must be.[3] To claim that X follows Y is to claim that X depends on Y in some way in which Y does not depend on X. Aristotle's point about *knowledge* was not just that we become aware that time has passed by realizing there has been change but also that we become aware that there has been change by realizing that time has passed (219^a7–8).[4] The kind of priority that is implied by the *following* relation is not, then, epistemological priority. Rather, the claim that X follows Y implies that certain important features of X are the way they are *because of* corresponding features of Y. Y is, we might say, explanatorily prior to X. Aristotle spells out what this amounts to, when he considers the feature of being continuous: 'for through (*dia*) the magnitude's being continuous, the change too is continuous but through the change, the time' (219^a12–13). His view is that though we may come to know that a certain magnitude is continuous by observing that a change over it is continuous, it is the continuity of the magnitude that explains the continuity of the change and not vice versa.

To understand this fully, we need to specify a bit more clearly what is meant by 'correspondence' here. What is it for a feature of Y to explain a *corresponding* feature of X? To claim that X follows Y is not merely to claim that features of Y explain analogous features of X. I shall argue that the *following* relation implies a deeper structural correspondence than this. A 'corresponding feature' is not just an analogous feature; it is

---

[3] I am grateful to Edward Hussey for pointing this out to me.

[4] Later in his account, he adds that we measure change by time and time by change and that we measure change by magnitude and magnitude by change 'for we say that the road is long if the journey is long and that the journey is long, if the road is; and the time is long if the change is, and the change is if the time is' (220^b29–32). (In this context, he even says that time *horizei* (defines, bounds) change and change, time—a remark to which I shall return in Ch. 6 below.)

an analogous feature *of corresponding parts*. The claim that X follows Y is the claim (i) that to every part of X there corresponds some particular part of Y and vice versa (with the precise nature of this correspondence depending on the particular X and Y in question) and (ii) that certain structural relations between the parts of X are explained by the fact that there are analogous structural relations between the *corresponding* parts of Y.

The precise nature of the correspondence between the parts of X and the parts of Y will depend on the particular X and Y in question. It is, for this reason, best explained by means of an example. Consider the relation between a spatial movement and the path of that movement. There is a sense in which each part of the movement corresponds to a particular part of the path: each part of the movement is *over* some particular part of the movement's path. Conversely, each part of the path corresponds to a particular part of the movement: each part of the path is *the path of* some part of the movement. To explain a structural feature of the movement by appealing to the fact that the movement follows the magnitude that is its path is to say (i) that the movement's parts correspond in this way to parts of its path (and the parts of its path correspond to parts of the movement) and (ii) that the movement's parts are structurally related in a certain way because the corresponding parts of the path are structurally related in an analogous way. For example, in the train journey from London to Leeds, the part of the journey that is through Doncaster is between the part that is through Peterborough and the part that is through Wakefield because, in the path of this journey, Doncaster is between Peterborough and Wakefield.

This sheds some light on what is meant by the claim that certain features of Y *correspond* to features of X, but it still leaves undetermined what exactly it is for a feature of Y to *explain* a corresponding feature of X. There are many different ways in which a feature of one thing might be said to explain a corresponding feature of another. The view could be that Y's possession of certain features is what makes it possible for X to have corresponding features. Or it could be that Y's possession of those features makes it necessary that X have those features. Moreover, the claim that X follows Y does not, by itself, tell us to what *extent* features of X are explained by corresponding features of Y. Is Aristotle claiming that the structural features of a change are entirely determined by the structure of the associated magnitude or is he making the more modest claim that some aspects of these features are explained by corresponding features of the magnitude? I discuss these questions below, when I look in more detail at the way in which Aristotle invokes relations of *following* to explain particular features of time, change, and magnitude.[5]

We can take a step towards understanding these relations of dependency by getting clearer about their *relata*. What is being said to explain what? Aristotle is making a claim here about the relations between *particular* times, changes, and magnitudes, not about the relation between time, change, and magnitude in general.[6] His claim is that a magnitude is explanatorily prior to a *change that is associated with the magnitude* and that a change is explanatorily prior to the *time of that change*.[7] But what does he mean here by 'magnitude' and by 'change'? And what is it for a change to be, in the relevant sense, *associated with* a certain magnitude?

'Magnitude' must, I think, mean 'spatial magnitude'. The magnitude over which a change occurs is a spatial path associated with the change. It is tempting to try to understand 'magnitude' in some broader, not exclusively spatial, sense. For instance, it might be thought that the magnitude associated with a qualitative change was the range of qualitative states through which the changing thing passed. On this view, when the sea changed gradually from dark blue to a lighter blue, the

---

[5] I discuss continuity in the second half of this chapter, and I discuss the before and after in the next chapter.

[6] The fact that he is not considering the relations between different changes explains his otherwise puzzling remark that 'the amount of time that has passed is always thought to be as much as the amount of change' (219ª13–14). Of course, this is not a general truth. If A is moving more quickly than B, then in the same period of time, A's movement will be greater than B's. He can make this remark only because he is thinking here of a single moving thing progressing at a uniform rate. His point is simply that in twice as much time, the moving thing will go twice as far. Philoponos and Aquinas both attribute much greater significance to this remark. They think that it shows that Aristotle is talking here only of the uniform motion of the outermost heavenly sphere and that it is *this* movement alone that time follows (Philoponos, *In Phys.* 719, 4–7, Aquinas, *Aristotle's Physics*, l.17, n. 576). But this cannot be right. Aristotle gives no indication that he is only talking of this primary movement. Moreover, his claim that the continuity of movement depends on the continuity of magnitude holds (if at all) quite generally, not only of the movement of the outermost sphere.

[7] Because of this, his claim that time follows change leaves unanswered certain important questions about the way in which one and the same time series is related to different changes. It does not, for instance, tell us anything about what it is for two different changes to be at the same time. Aristotle's account of this depends on his view that time is a kind of number (a view I shall discuss in Part 3).

magnitude along which it changed would be the spectrum of lighter and lighter shades of blue. But this interpretation is ruled out by Aristotle's denial elsewhere that qualitative states come in infinitely many different degrees. (In the *De Sensu*, for example, he argues that there are only finitely many different shades of colour.)[8] Since one of his claims in our passage is that the continuity (that is, the infinite divisibility) of change depends on the continuity of an associated magnitude, the magnitude to which he is referring must be of a kind to be infinitely divisible. This strongly suggests that in his remarks here he is speaking only of *spatial* magnitude.

But if this is right, should we understand him to be using the word 'change' (*kinēsis*) in a similarly narrow sense, to refer only to *spatial movement*? There are two reasons for thinking we should not. The first is that, in the immediate context of these remarks about following, Aristotle is clearly using the word 'change' in its broader sense. These remarks come just after the argument that there can be no time without change. This is an argument that there can be no time unless there is *some kind of change or other*, not that there can be no time without spatial movement. To claim that whenever we think that time has passed, we think there has also been a change (219^a7-8), is not to claim that in all such cases we think there has been a spatial movement.[9] The second reason for thinking that the word 'change' should be understood more broadly is that Aristotle uses it in this broader sense in a closely related passage earlier in the *Physics*. In his account of the infinite in *Physics* III, he claims that time is infinite because change is and change is infinite because magnitude is.[10] Here, though, he adds explicitly that by 'change' he means not only locomotion, but also qualitative change:

The infinite is not the same in magnitude and in change and in time, as being one nature, but the posterior is said to be in accordance with (*kata*) the prior, for

---

[8] *De Sensu*, 6. $445^b20-446^a20$.

[9] A sign that he means 'change' to be understood in a broad sense is his willingness to use '*metabolē*' and '*kinēsis*' interchangeably in this passage. (Elsewhere, '*metabolē*' is used not just for movements and alterations, but also for coming to be and passing away, *Physics* V.1.225^a34-^b3.) Note that he says explicitly in the last sentence of ch. 10 (218^b19-20) that they can, for present purposes, be used interchangeably.

[10] There are difficulties in interpreting this passage. Does he simply mean 'infinitely divisible'? But then time and change are also infinite in another sense: they go on forever. And yet he has made it quite clear that he does not think spatial magnitude can be infinite in the sense of infinitely *extended*.

example, the change is [said to be infinite] because the magnitude is along which something changes or alters qualitatively or grows, but the time is [said to be infinite] because the change is. $(207^b21–5)$

I have argued that by 'magnitude' Aristotle means spatial magnitude, whereas by 'change' he means not only locomotion but also other kinds of change. This raises a question. There is an obvious connection between a spatial movement and a certain spatial path: the movement is *along* a certain path. Moreover, as a growing thing increases in size, a point on its surface will trace out a spatial path. But in what way are qualitative changes related to spatial paths? An answer, at least with regard to *certain* qualitative changes, is suggested by Aristotle's discussion of continuity in the fourth and fifth chapters of *Physics* VI.[11] He claims there that a qualitative change is infinitely divisible only accidentally and that its infinite divisibility is explained by the divisibility of the changing thing.[12] The thought seems to be that in a qualitative change a new property spreads gradually through the changing thing. The change is continuous because the spreading of the new property is continuous and the spreading of the new property is continuous because the thing through which it is spreading (i.e. the changing thing) is continuous. For example, if the sea is becoming paler, it is the infinite divisibility of the sea that makes this change infinitely divisible. When the sea becomes paler, each minimal change (from one shade of blue to the next) spreads continuously over the surface of the sea.[13] The change in colour is continuous because each of the spreadings of colour over the surface is continuous. And these are continuous because they each trace out a continuous spatial path. If this is right, then the structure of this colour-change depends on the structure of spatial magnitude in an

---

[11] I owe this explanation of the dependence of qualitative change on magnitude to Hussey (1993: 143).

[12] *Physics* VI.4.235ᵃ17–18, 235ᵃ34–36 and 5.236ᵇ2–8. Cf. *Generation and Corruption* II.10.337ᵃ27–30, where Aristotle says that the continuity of change depends, in general, on the continuity of the changing thing, since a property can only be continuous in virtue of the continuity of the thing to which it belongs.

[13] Aristotle says here that while something is undergoing one of these minimal changes, part of it must be in the state it is leaving and part of it must be in the state it is changing to. For example, if the sea is changing between a light shade of blue and the next darker shade of blue, part of the sea must be in the lighter shade and part of it must be in the darker shade, *Physics* VI.4.234ᵇ10–20. Note that the changes in question are the *minimal* changes, so the claim is not refuted by the fact that changes in colour sometimes do not *appear* to occur in this way.

indirect way: the colour-change is continuous, because an associated spatial movement is continuous.

However, in spite of what he says in these chapters of *Physics* VI, it is hard to believe that Aristotle would defend the view that *every* qualitative change involves the spreading of some new quality through a changing thing. (It would be very odd, for instance, to think that this was true of the change: *becoming musical.*) In fact, he himself contradicts this general claim later in the *Physics*. In *Physics* VIII, he says that the fact that the changing thing is infinitely divisible need not imply that the change is so too: a body of water can freeze all at once (3.253^{b}23–6). This suggests that his considered view is not that *all* qualitative changes depend for their structure on associated spatial movements, but only that certain qualitative changes are structurally dependent in this way. Those changes in which a new quality spreads through the changing thing will have a structure that depends on the structure of this spreading movement (and hence, on the structure of this movement's spatial path).

I have argued that the main point Aristotle is making, when he claims that change follows magnitude, is that the structure of a spatial movement depends on that of its path. But because of the way in which certain other kinds of change are related to spatial movement, in making this claim, he is also saying something about these other kinds of change. In those cases in which the structure of a qualitative change itself depends on the structure of a spatial movement, the structure of this qualitative change will also depend (though in an indirect way) on the structure of a certain spatial path.

This helps us to understand what Aristotle means by the claim that time follows change and change follows magnitude. But what are his grounds for believing this claim? He presents it here without argument. He does argue elsewhere for a *correspondence* between the structural features of time, change, and magnitude. In Book VI, for instance, he tries to show that if movement is continuous, time and spatial magnitude must be (2.232^{b}20–233^{a}12). But he nowhere explicitly defends his assumptions about *priority*: the assumptions that features of time depend on those of change and that the features of change depend on those of an associated magnitude.

It is perhaps not surprising that he takes it for granted that change is prior in this way to time. After all, he has already committed himself to

the view that time is 'something of change'. If time is essentially
something dependent on change, then it is at least natural to assume
that, in the cases in which there is a correspondence between features of
time and features of change, the features of time will be explained by the
corresponding features of change. He does not have the same reason for
thinking that magnitude is explanatorily prior to change. After all,
change is not defined as 'something of magnitude'. Why, then, does
he claim that it is the path that is explanatorily prior to the movement
rather than vice versa? There is no direct answer to this in the text, so
we can only speculate. There are, I think, two different reasons he
might give. First, he could point out that though any spatial movement
must be over some magnitude or other (it must, as he says, be a
movement 'from something to something', 219^{a}10–11), there can be
spatial magnitudes over which nothing moves.[14] This shows that there
is at least one respect in which a spatial path is prior to a movement over
it. Aristotle could be taking this as an indication that the path is also
explanatorily prior to the movement. Second, he might add that though
there can be many different movements over one and the same path, one
(token) movement cannot have two different paths. This makes it
natural to assume that, if there is a structural correspondence between
the path and the movements over it, it is the structure of the path that
determines that of the movements, and not vice versa.[15]

Aristotle makes only these few remarks about *following*. I have raised
questions both about what they mean and about how they might be
defended. The text does not provide us with enough evidence to settle
these questions decisively, but we can get somewhat further by looking
in more detail at the particular features that he explains by means of the
following relations. In the remainder of this chapter, I discuss his claims

[14] There is a complication here, arising from Aristotle's views about continuity.
Aristotle thinks that for a path over a continuous surface to be, it must be marked out
in some way, so we cannot just assume that any possible path of a movement will exist
prior to that movement. However, it is possible for a path to be marked out from its
surroundings without anything ever moving along it. An example is the line that is the
edge of my desk. This would be differentiated from its surroundings whether or not
anything ever moved along it.
[15] There is, it must be admitted, an obvious objection to this. An analogous consid-
eration would lead one to suppose that time was explanatorily prior to change. Any token
change is at one and only one time, but there can be many different changes at the same
time. Nevertheless, it is a basic assumption of Aristotle's whole account that time is
something that depends on change.

about continuity. In Chapter 4, I turn to his more difficult remarks about the before and after.

CONTINUITY

In this context, to say that time is continuous is to say that between any two instants (or 'nows' as Aristotle calls them) there can always be another instant.[16] Aristotle's contention, then, is that time has this structure because certain changes are continuous (between any two instants of a change there can always be another instant of change)[17] and that these changes have this structure because spatial magnitude does (between any two points on a line, there can always be another point).[18]

As we shall see, the arguments that establish these claims depend upon there being a correspondence between the parts of a spatial movement and the parts of its path, and also between the parts of a spatial movement and the parts of the time of that movement. Each part of the movement is over some part of the path and each part of the path has some part of the movement that is over it. Similarly, each part of the time is the time of some part of the movement and each part of the movement occurs during some part of the time. (Or, equivalently, each potential division in the movement marks out a potential division in its path and vice versa, and each potential division in the time marks out a potential division in the movement and vice versa.) This is just the kind of correspondence that I have claimed must hold between the parts of X and the parts of Y if X is to follow Y.[19]

Aristotle holds that the continuity of a spatial movement is both made possible and ensured by the continuity of its path. The claim

---

[16] The definition of 'continuous' that he is using here is: 'divisible into parts that are always further divisible' (*Physics* VI.2.232^{b}24–5).

[17] The difference between a *temporal* instant and an instant of change is brought out by the fact that an instant of a change is defined with reference to the change in question. There can be many different instants of change at one and the same temporal instant. For change-instants to be simultaneous is for them to be at one and the same temporal instant.

[18] Strictly speaking, the path of a moving thing will be three-dimensional. But if a line is infinitely divisible in the way I have described, a three-dimensional path will be so too: between any two cross sections of the path there can always be another one.

[19] See above, p. 48–9.

about *making possible* depends on the idea that the path provides the possible stages for a movement over it. For example, in a movement over the line ABC, there can be a stage *being-at-B* between the stages *being-at-A* and *being-at-C* just because there can be a point B between the points A and C.[20] From the fact that the movement from A to C is divisible, it follows that the distance AC must also be divisible. To divide the movement between A and C is just to stop the movement when the moving thing has only moved over *part* of the distance AC.

Of course, there is a way in which we could pick out the stages of a movement without referring to its path. We could use different times in the movement to distinguish between its stages. Half way through the time of the movement would be the stage of the movement's being half over, a quarter of the way through would be the stage of its being a quarter over, and so on. But Aristotle's view about the relation between time and change implies that in order to do this we would have to appeal to the divisibility of some *other* movement that was going on at the same time. The reason for this is that the times themselves are only distinguished from each other because they are at earlier and later stages in movements. What ensures that a movement is infinitely divisible in its own right (and not just that we can make accidental divisions in it by referring to its relations to other movements) is that its path is infinitely divisible.[21]

The other part of Aristotle's claim is that the continuity of the path *ensures* the continuity of the movement over it. This depends on his view that it is not possible for something to 'jump' from being at one place to being at another, distant place (*Physics* VI.1, especially 231ᵇ28–232ᵃ1). He never really argues for this view. He takes it for granted that in going from one place to another, a moving thing must traverse some path, and that, to do so, it must pass through whatever points are on this path.

It is interesting to note that whatever plausibility there is in this assumption depends entirely on the fact that we are talking here about the relation between a spatial movement and its path. We feel no

---

[20] I say '*can be* a point' and '*can be* a stage' because of Aristotle's view that points on a line and instantaneous change-stages only exist in so far as they are marked out in some way. (See Introduction, p. 9–13.)

[21] As I have already explained, the fact that a qualitative change cannot be infinitely divisible in its own right is Aristotle's reason for saying that such a change is only *accidentally* infinitely divisible (*Physics* VI.4.235ᵃ34–6, see above, p. 52).

analogous temptation to think that in passing from one pitch to another a sound must glissando through all the intermediate pitches, or that in changing from white to black something must pass through all the intermediate shades of grey. This reflects, I think, an interesting difference between the relation of a spatial movement to its path and the relation of a qualitative movement to the range of states it is a movement through. When something passes from one point to another, there must be something else that occupies the space in between.[22] It is natural to think that the spatial structure of this *something else* determines the structure of the movement. Consider, for instance, a stone that is moving through water. The water exists independently of the stone and has its own spatial structure. We can understand, then, why it might be plausible to suppose that the infinite divisibility of the water is what explains the infinite divisibility of the movement through it. In contrast, for a violin to make first a sound of one pitch and then a sound of another pitch, it need stand in no special relation to anything else that is already making sounds of those two pitches or of the pitches in between. There is, we might say, no independently existing medium that the violin has to 'pass through' in going from one pitch to another, as the stone has to pass through the water to get from one place to another. Because of this, there is no temptation to think that the structure of a change in pitch is constrained by something else, in the way that Aristotle supposes the structure of a spatial movement is constrained by its path.

Aristotle's reason for providing an explanation of the continuity of change is that this in its turn explains the continuity of time. Time is continuous just because some continuous change or other is always going on.[23] The claim that a change can only be continuous if its time is can easily be justified by appealing to certain plausible Aristotelian assumptions. Aristotle has already argued that there can be no change without time (218^b21–219^a10). If there were a distinction

---

[22] At least, on *Aristotle's* view there must be something that occupies this space in between, since he thinks that there is no empty space. (He defends this view that there is no such thing as void in *Physics* IV. 6–9.)

[23] Some continuous change will always be going on because there will always be spatial movement (and spatial movement is continuous). That there will always be spatial movement is guaranteed by the fact that some spatial movements (the movements of the heavenly spheres) go on forever. (He argues that there are such eternal movements in *Physics* VIII.7–9.)

between an earlier and a later stage of a change without a corresponding distinction between earlier and later times, then the changing thing would, in going from the earlier to the later stage, accomplish a change in no time at all.[24] Since this is impossible, there must be at least as many potential divisions between times within a period as there are between the stages of a change that is going on during that period. It follows that an infinitely divisible change must take place in an infinitely divisible period of time.

This explains why Aristotle thinks that if there is an infinitely divisible movement, its time must also be infinitely divisible. Is it also true that the existence of infinitely divisible movements is a *necessary* condition for the infinite divisibility of time? From the fact that earlier and later times are only distinct from one another in virtue of the different change-stages that are at them, it follows that time will only be infinitely divisible if there can be a distinct change-stage between any two non-simultaneous change-stages. But it might be objected that this in itself is not enough to show that the infinite divisibility of time presupposes the infinite divisibility of change. Even if all changes were composed of indivisible phases, they could nevertheless fit together in such a way that between any two potential divisions in changes there was always a potential division in some *other* change.

Aristotle does not consider this possible objection. But perhaps it is not an objection that he would find too troubling. He would say, I think, that if temporal continuity depended on the way in which different changes *happened* to fit together then its basis would be purely accidental. Though it is theoretically possible that this should happen, if it did, the continuity of time would be, in a certain sense, inexplicable.[25] A genuine explanation of this continuity must appeal to the fact that

---

[24] Clearly, something cannot be at both an earlier and a later stage of a change at one and the same temporal instant. Instantaneous changes, if they can occur, happen when something *has changed* to a certain state without ever *having been in process of changing* to that state, not when something is in two different states at one and the same instant.

[25] Compare his remarks on coincidence in *Metaphysics* VI.3 and *Physics* II.4–6. The occurrence of a certain coincidence may be necessitated by previous chains of events, but that is not to say that its occurrence has a causal explanation. See Sorabji (1980: ch. 1).

there are always continuous changes. There is nothing else that could provide a non-accidental basis for the continuity of time. For Aristotle, the fact that time is continuous must be explicable, because it is a fact that holds universally: all time is continuous. Something that is universal in this way cannot, he thinks, just be founded on accident.[26]

---

[26] Cf. his argument against Empedocles in *Physics* II.8, which relies on the claim that things that happen always or for the most part cannot be accidental (198^{b}34–6).

4

The Before and After

Aristotle also invokes the relation of *following* to explain what he calls 'the before and after' (219^a14–19). Some explanation of what it is to be before or after is obviously needed in any account of time. In Aristotle's account, this explanation is of particular importance, as he is going to define time as 'a number of change with respect to the before and after' (219^b1–2). This definition will not be very informative unless he also has something to say about what it is to be before or after.

But at this crucial point, he says frustratingly little. Such explanation as he gives, draws once again upon the relations between time, change, and magnitude. The before and after is, he tells us, first of all in place. (In this context, 'place' seems to be just another word for spatial magnitude.) Because there is a before and after in place, there is a before and after in change, and because there is a before and after in change, there is a before and after in time. As he puts it:

Therefore, the before and after is first of all in place. And there it is in position. But since the before and after is in magnitude, it is necessary that also the before and after is in change, by analogy with the things there. But the before and after is also in time, through the following always of the one upon the other of them. (219^a14–19)

We are left to speculate about what exactly he supposes these different types of before and after to be and how he thinks they are related to one another.

It is not even clear quite what Aristotle is trying to achieve in this passage. Is it an attempt to give an account of temporal asymmetry in terms of some other more basic kind of asymmetry, as a modern causal account of time might try to explain temporal order in terms of some more basic kind of causal order? Or are his aims much more modest?

Is he, for instance, claiming only that different times, like positions on a line, form a linear series?

Our first task must be to understand what these different kinds of before and after are. Aristotle describes various different kinds of before and after, including those in time, in change, and in place, in his philosophical dictionary in *Metaphysics* V.[1] We cannot assume that he is using exactly the same notions of before and after in our section of the *Physics* (and indeed, I shall argue that he is not), but since he does at least give some account of these terms in the *Metaphysics*, it will be helpful to look at what he says there.

In reading the *Metaphysics* account, it is useful to bear in mind that the words *proteron* and *husteron* that I have been translating 'before' and 'after' also have what in English is the slightly wider meaning of *prior* and *posterior*. Thus, in the *Metaphysics*, the most basic kind of *proteron* and *husteron* is not temporal. It is, rather, what Aristotle calls the 'before and after in nature and substance'. (X is before Y in nature and substance just in case X can exist without Y but Y cannot exist without X.)

Aristotle groups together the before and afters in time, in change, and in place as all being of the same general type. Each of them, he says, is defined relative to some origin. We call things before and after in time, change, or place, 'because they are nearer some beginning determined either *simpliciter* and by nature, or in relation to some thing or some place, or by certain people' (*Metaphysics* V. 11 1018^{b}10–12). Thus, to be before or after in place is to be nearer to or further from some place that is the origin. Aristotle says that this origin might be fixed by nature (it might, for example, be the middle or the end of something), or it might be defined with reference to some chance object. Something is before in place if it is nearer to the place that is the origin; something is after in place if it is further from the origin. To be before or after in change is to be nearer to or further from what Aristotle calls the 'first mover'. The boy, he says, is before the man in change. Presumably, in this case the first mover is the father[2] and the boy is before the grown man

---

[1] And also, though less fully, in *Categories* 12. However, in the *Categories* he says that the before and after in time is the most primary kind of before and after.

[2] See, for instance, *Metaphysics* IX, 8.1049^{b}24–7: 'for what actually is always comes to be from what potentially is, on account of what is actual, e.g. man from man, musician from musician, there always being some first mover, and the mover already existing actually'.

because the boy is (in some sense) closer to his father than the grown man is. For time, the relevant origin is the present. Thus, to be before or after in time is to be nearer to or further from the present. But in this case a slight complication must be introduced into the account. In the future, what is before is nearer to the present, but in the past what is before is further from the present. The Trojan wars are prior to the Persian wars because they are further from the present, but tomorrow's exam is before next week's holiday, because the exam is nearer to the present.[3]

These remarks in the *Metaphysics* are very brief and leave much unexplained, but they provide a useful starting point for our investigation of the before and after in the *Physics*. We are now in a position to ask about the relation between Aristotle's account of time and these definitions from *Metaphysics* V.11. I shall look at each of the three kinds of before and after in turn.

THE BEFORE AND AFTER IN TIME

The account Aristotle gives of the temporal before and after in the *Physics* is quite different from the account he gives in the *Metaphysics*. There is a certain sense in which the two accounts view time from different perspectives. As we shall see, the *Metaphysics* account is a view of time *as from some particular present*, whereas the account in the *Physics* is a view of time *as it is passing*.

In the *Metaphysics*, Aristotle presents what I shall call a 'present-relative' view of temporal order. It is a view that defines the temporal 'before' and 'after' in terms of distance from the present. This view is striking both because of the central role it accords to the present and because it makes temporal order depend upon duration (upon 'distance' from the present). Because of the reference to the present, it is, in a certain sense, a static account of the before and after in time. It describes temporal order as from some particular present and tells us nothing about the relation between this order and temporal order as from some other present. One consequence of this is that the *Metaphysics* account of what it is to be temporally before or after is completely divorced from any account of *how we know* that one thing is temporally before or after

[3] *Metaphysics* V.11.

another. Typically, when we perceive a change, we know in an immediate way that we perceive one stage of the change before we perceive another stage.[4] We know this without calculating distances from the present. Indeed, our knowledge depends on the fact that since the perceiving itself takes time, the present at which we perceive one stage of a change will not be the same as the present at which we perceive another.

Aristotle's primary account in the *Physics*, unlike the *Metaphysics* account, takes as its starting point our awareness of the passing of time. After describing the way in which time follows change, he immediately goes on to point out that we are aware that time has passed whenever we perceive a before and after order in a change (219ª22–5). When we mark out these different stages of a change, he says, we mark out two different nows, one of them temporally before the other (219ª25–9). There is no mention here of the relative distances of change-stages from the now. Rather, Aristotle's account depends on the fact that, as something changes, different stages of the change are, successively, now. This is an account of time, *as it is passing*, not an account of time *as from some fixed present*.

The *Physics* account also appeals to our activity in marking out time, in a way that the present-relative account cannot do. We cannot mark out temporal order by measuring the distance of different events from the present, since there would be no *one* present that lasted for the length of time it took us to do the measuring. In his account of time in the *Physics*, Aristotle makes use of the fact that we mark the present *as it passes*. Each present we mark will be different from the one before. The series of presents, or nows, that we mark out in this way is the before and after in time: 'when . . . the soul says that the nows are two, the one before and the other after, then it is and this it is that we say is time' (219ª27–9). Whether *things in time* are temporally before or after one another depends on their relation to the series of nows. For example, the Trojan war is temporally before the Persian war because the nows that mark out the beginning and end of the Trojan war are before the nows that mark out the beginning and end of the Persian war.[5]

---

[4] Of course, we can be mistaken about this. We can be under the illusion that one stage is before another in some change (as happens in the waterfall illusion). My point is only that *if* we know that one stage leads up to another in some change we know immediately that the one is temporally before the other.

[5] Of course, there is considerable idealization involved in thinking of a war as beginning and ending at different *instants*.

I have claimed that this is Aristotle's primary view in the *Physics*. However, it must be admitted that he does also refer to the *Metaphysics'* present-relative view in some remarks towards the end of his account (*Physics* IV.14.222^{b}30–223^{a}15). The context is an argument that every change is in time. Changes, he says, can be faster or slower. A faster change is one that reaches its end state *before* another (over the same extension and with the same kind of change). From this, he claims, it follows that all changes are in time, since the 'before' mentioned here is a temporal before. It is in defending the claim that this 'before' is temporal that he appeals to the present-relative view of temporal order. He argues that, since the before and after are spoken of with reference to distance from the now and the now itself is in time, the before and after must be in time too.

There is, of course, much that is questionable about this argument.[6] But for our purposes, its main interest lies in its appeal to the present-relative view of time. That Aristotle should refer to this view here is puzzling and he says nothing to make it less so. Is he presenting this view as an alternative to his primary account? He gives no indication that he is. But in that case, what exactly is the relation between the view that defines the temporal before and after as from the present and the view that defines it in terms of an order that we mark out as time passes? On the face of it, the two accounts are very different.[7] What reason is there to suppose they both define one and the same temporal order? None of these are questions that Aristotle answers. His allusion to the present-relative view here is intriguing, but it is only an allusion. He does nothing to integrate this view into his overall account.[8]

---

[6] The account of faster and slower in terms of reaching the end of the change does not (or at least does not straightforwardly) apply to changes that go on forever. Are these changes too 'in time'? Even if the 'before' that is mentioned in the account of faster and slower is the temporal *before*, does it follow that the changes themselves are in time? Is the sense in which the change is in time the same as the sense in which the before and after and the now are in time?

[7] It is worth noting that the two views each raise different problems about temporal unity. On the present-relative view, some account is needed of the relation between time as defined from one present and time as defined from another. On the other view, something needs to be said about the relation between the temporal order that we mark when we mark the before and after in one change and the temporal order that we mark when we mark the before and after in another.

[8] For an interpretation that attributes much greater significance to these remarks see Broadie (1984).

THE BEFORE AND AFTER IN CHANGE

As we have seen, the before and after in time depends in some way upon a more basic before and after in change. Again, there is very little, in the *Physics*, to indicate what Aristotle means by the 'before and after in change'. Even the account in *Metaphysics* V leaves many questions unanswered. According to that account, to be before or after in change is to be nearer to or further from the first mover of the change, as the boy is nearer to his father than is the grown man. But do all changes have first movers that stand to them as the father stands to this change? How is this account to apply to eternal changes? Surely, no stage of the rotation of the outermost sphere is closer to its first mover than any other. What, in any case, is it to be 'closer' to the first mover of a change? Does Aristotle simply mean 'closer in time' (in which case, at least according to this *Metaphysics* account, the before and after in change depends in an important way on the before and after in time)?

A consequence of defining the before and after in a change in terms of distance from the first mover of the change is that there is no *one* series: *the* before and after in change. 'The before and after in change' is a general way of referring to several before-and-after series: a different one for each particular change. Moreover, there is no one relation of *before in change* or of *after in change*. The relations of *before in change* and of *after in change* are defined relative to the change in question. Thus, there is one relation which is the relation of *being before in the growth of this boy into a man* and there is another relation that is the relation of *being before in the flight of the arrow that killed King Harold*. Each of these relations defines a before and after series. The first defines the before and after series of the stages of the growth of this boy into a man; the second defines the before and after series of the stages in the flight of the Harold-killing arrow.

When he mentions the before and after in change in the *Physics*, Aristotle says nothing about the first mover of the change. But there is some reason to suppose that here too he is thinking of the before and after in a change as a series that is defined relative to a particular change. His one explanatory remark, when he introduces the notion of the before and after in change, concerns its relation to change. He says, cryptically, that the before and after in change is 'that, whatever it is, by being which change is, but its being is different and not change' (219^{a}20–1).^{9} In claiming that the before and after in change is 'that by being which change is', he is making it clear just how close the relationship is between the before and after in a change and the change in question. The before and after in a change is the series of earlier and later stages in the change. Though this series of earlier and later stages is not identical to the change ('its being is different'), it provides what we might call the *structure* of the change. It is in virtue of having this structure (in virtue of being divisible into this before and after series) that the change is the change it is.

Aristotle's doctrine, in the *Physics*, that time follows change places an important constraint on our understanding of 'the before and after in change'. As we have seen, he holds that the various series of before and afters in changes are explanatorily prior to the before and after in time. It is natural to understand this as the claim that if a certain stage P is before another stage Q in a change then, because of this, P is temporally before Q.^{10} But if this is his view, then he needs some non-temporal account of the before and after in change. That is, he needs an account of what it is for one stage to be before another in a change that doesn't depend upon the notion of being temporally before. For instance, the account of what it is for a stage P to be before another stage Q in the movement that is the flight of the Harold-killing arrow *cannot* be: (i) stage P is temporally before stage Q and (ii) stage P and stage Q are both stages in the movement of the Harold-killing arrow.^{11} The question whether he can give such a non-temporal account of the before and after in change will be central to the remainder of this chapter. Since his view is not just that time follows change, but also that change follows place (or magnitude), there is reason to think that if he has such an account, it

---

^{9} The odd expression 'that, whatever it is, by being which change is' is my translation of the Greek 'ho men pote on kinēsis [esti]'. I discuss the Greek phrase 'ho pote on X esti' in the Appendix.
   ^{10} This is not an attempt to give a *full* explanation of the before in time in terms of the before in change. He says nothing here about the temporal relations between stages of *different* changes.
   ^{11} In this respect, Aristotle faces a challenge something like that faced by the modern causal theorist of time. The modern causal theorist has the analogous problem of finding a non-temporal distinction between cause and effect. But the challenge for Aristotle might seem more difficult. How could there possibly be a non-temporal account of the distinction between before and after in a change?

will make reference to the before and after in place. Our next task, then, must be to work out what he means here by 'the before and after in place'.

THE BEFORE AND AFTER IN PLACE

In our passage of the *Physics*, Aristotle writes both of the before and after in place and of the before and after 'in magnitude'. He says that the before and after is first of all in place, and then adds that, since the before and after is 'in magnitude' it is also in change. As I have already said, he is, I think, simply using the terms 'in magnitude' and 'in place' interchangeably. We can understand why it is natural for him to do so, if we assume that he is sticking closely here to the account of the before and after in place that he gives in the *Metaphysics*. On that account, if one position P1 is before another position P2 in place, then the distance from P1 to some place that is the origin is less than the distance from P2 to that origin. In other words, the *magnitude* of the line joining P1 to the origin will be smaller than the magnitude of the line joining P2 to the origin.

I have already said that there is no one relation of before in change. Rather there is a relation *before in this change* and a different relation *before in that change*. Similarly, this account of the before and after in place implies that there is no one relation *before in place*. What is before (or after) in place is before (or after) *relative to a particular origin*.

There is also, I think, a further complication to Aristotle's view of the before and after in place. To be before or after in place is not just to be before or after relative to a particular origin, but also to be before or after *along a particular path*. By a 'path' in this context, I simply mean a line extending from the origin through the two positions that are before and after and ending at some place other than the origin.[12] A position P1 might be nearer to the origin O than another position P2 along one path, but further away along some other, more roundabout path. That is, P1 might be *before* P2 from the origin O along one path but *after* it

---

[12] A path that is a closed loop will not provide the basis for a before and after relation, since along such a path, if point P2 is nearer to the origin than point P1 in one direction then point P1 will be nearer to the origin in the other direction. Whether this implies that the stages of a circular change cannot be before or after in that change is a question to which I return below (p. 76, n.23).

along another path. Along any one path, there will be two possible *before* relations, corresponding to the two different origins of the path. If P1 is before P2 on a certain path relative to the origin O, then P2 will be before P1 relative to the origin that is at the other end of the path.

In claiming that to be before or after in place is to be before or after along a particular path, I am going beyond anything that Aristotle himself actually says. Assuming that this is what he means will make it easier to make sense of his remarks about the relation between the before and after in place and the before and after in change. But there is also some basis for this view in the *Metaphysics* chapter on the before and after.[13] I have already mentioned that Aristotle claims, in this chapter, that there is a primary kind of before and after, which he calls the before and after in 'substance and nature'. X is before Y in substance and nature if and only if X can exist without Y but Y cannot exist without X ($1019^a2–4$). The example he gives is that a part line is before the whole line in respect of destruction, since a part can continue to exist when the whole has been destroyed, though the whole cannot continue to exist when the part has been destroyed.[14] At the end of the chapter, he says that the different kinds of before and after he has described are all connected to this primary kind of before and after ($1019^a11–12$). If the before and after in place is defined, as I have suggested it should be, as along a certain path and relative to a certain origin, then its connection to the primary kind of before and after is quite straightforward. To see this consider the path ABC:

A————————————B————————————C

Relative to the origin A and along this path, point B is before point C in place if and only if the line AB is a proper part of the line AC. That is, relative to the origin A and along this path, B is before C in place if and

---

[13] On the other hand, it might be argued that the fact that one of Aristotle's examples of an origin is 'the middle' (1018^b13) suggests that he is not thinking of the origin as being at one end of some path. (One natural way to understand 'the middle' is as referring to the centre of a circle.)

[14] There is a sense in which the whole could exist without the part, since the whole could exist even if the part had not been marked out in it. But Aristotle must be presupposing that the part in question here has been marked out in some way.

only if the line AB is before the line AC in nature and substance (in respect of destruction).[15]

THE RELATIONS BETWEEN THE BEFORE AND AFTERS IN PLACE, CHANGE, AND TIME: IS ARISTOTLE'S ACCOUNT CIRCULAR?

Aristotle's reason for mentioning these different kinds of before and after in the *Physics* is to provide some non-temporal basis for the before and after in time. Now that we have discussed what the different sorts of before and after might be we can start to think more carefully about the relations between them. In what sense does Aristotle think he is providing an explanation of the before and after in time? And can he provide some account of the before or after in change that does not presuppose a prior account of temporal order?

Many of his readers have complained that he cannot. Their complaint is based on one natural interpretation of what he is saying in this passage. Consider, for instance, a line AB, a movement over the line, and the time taken by this movement.

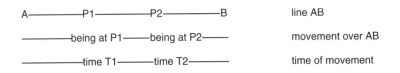

According to this interpretation, Aristotle is deriving temporal asymmetry from an asymmetrical relation between the stages in a movement and he is deriving this relation between the stages in a movement from a more basic asymmetrical relation between positions on a line. His view is that there is a basic before and after relation on the line AB. Say, P1 is

---

[15] Of course, this does not tell us how the before and afters in change and in time are related to the before and after in nature and substance. But if, as Aristotle claims in the *Physics*, time follows change and change follows place, then perhaps the relation of the before and after in nature and substance to the before and after in place can be used to explain its relation to these other two kinds of before and after.

before P2 on the line AB. Because of this, *being at P1* is before (rather than after) *being at P2* in the movement from A to B. Because of this, *the time of being at P1* is temporally before (rather than after) *the time of being at P2.*

If this is Aristotle's view, then it is indeed flawed. To see why, it is only necessary to reflect on the fact that the relation of before in place is always relative to an origin. While P1 is before P2 relative to the origin A, it is after P2 relative to the origin B. The question then arises: which origin is relevant in this case? The easiest answer is that the origin is the point from which the movement starts. But this answer would imply that what was before on the line depended on what was before in the change, rather than vice versa. Alternatively, there could be some independent reason why one end of the line rather than the other was the origin. (Perhaps such a reason can be found by appealing to some of Aristotle's weirder views about place—for example his view that the universe has an absolute right and left and that right is prior to left.)[16] But this won't do either. For suppose that A were, for some such reason, the origin of this line. This would have the absurd consequence that any movement over the line would have to be in the direction from A to B.

This argument has led most interpreters to claim that Aristotle's account of temporal order either has obviously false consequences or is viciously circular.[17] Owen, for instance, says:

Now if temporal order is to be explained by the order of motion on...a line,... evidently the motion must have a direction.... But can this direction be derived from the spatial before-and-after we have just defined, without importing just the temporal priority we meant to explain? Evidently not.[18]

---

[16] *De Caelo* II.2, *Physics* IV.1.208^{b}14–19.

[17] Even if there were some way out of this dilemma, the proposed account would not work for any movement that involved traversing the same path twice, such as, for example, the movement a runner would make in going twice round a race track. Such a runner would be at the same spatial position at an earlier point in the movement and then again at a later point in the movement. Presumably this spatial position cannot be before itself in place! So the fact that being at this position for the first time is before being at it for the second time in the change cannot be explained by appealing, in the way that the proposed interpretation suggests, to the before and after in place. In fact, the account will not work for any circular movement, unless an account of the before and after in place can be developed that (unlike the account I have described) allows there to be a before and after in place along a circular path.

[18] Owen (1976: 313). Much the same criticism is made by Sorabji (1983: 86) and by Corish (1976: 245–51).

The fact that this view is so obviously unsatisfactory should lead us to question the interpretation that attributes it to Aristotle. One alternative interpretation is to deny that his aim here is to explain temporal asymmetry. Perhaps he is not giving an account of why it is that one time is before rather than after another. He could merely be claiming that the linear order of the series of points on a line is inherited by the order of the corresponding series of stages in a movement over that line and that this order is in its turn passed on to the series of instants in the time of this movement.[19] If this is all that he is saying, then his comments about the before and after add very little to the remarks he has already made about continuity.

This very modest interpretation is, I think, compatible with the text. It gives Aristotle a view that is somewhat unsatisfying for a modern reader, but this is not necessarily a reason to reject it. We are used to thinking that explaining temporal asymmetry is a central task for the philosophy of time. Because of this, it is easy to be disappointed by an interpretation on which Aristotle is not even attempting to give such an explanation. But we cannot be confident that Aristotle shared our assumptions about what is important. This would, in fact, not be the only point at which his account failed to address questions that seem to us to be central. (As we shall see, he has nothing that we would recognize as an account of simultaneity.) Indeed, one of the main obstacles to our understanding of Aristotle's discussion of time is that he differs so radically from us in his assumptions about what questions such an account needs to answer.[20]

Nevertheless, there is, I think, an alternative, more promising interpretation, which gives Aristotle something to say about temporal asymmetry but avoids saddling him with a view that is obviously circular. Though rooted in the text, the interpretation I shall propose is more speculative than the others I have considered, but the view it attributes to Aristotle is rich and interesting enough to be worth discussing in some detail.

---

[19] The linear order that was inherited in this way would be fully describable in terms of a relation of *between*.
[20] As I explained above in the Introduction, pp. 4–5.

EXPLAINING THE BEFORE AND AFTER IN CHANGE BY MEANS OF AN ANALOGY

The central claim of this interpretation is that the way in which the before and after in place is related to the before and after in change is quite different from the way in which the before and after in change is related to the before and after in time. Some support for this claim can be drawn from the words Aristotle uses to describe these relations of dependency. It is helpful here to look back at exactly what he says. He tells us that there is a before and after in time *because time follows change* ('because of the following always of one upon the other of them'). But when he talks about the before and after in change, he says that there is a before and after in change as well as in place, *because of an analogy between change and place* ('by analogy with the things there'):

> Therefore, the before and after is first of all in place. And there it is in position. But since the before and after is in magnitude, it is necessary that also the before and after is in change, by analogy with the things there. But the before and after is also in time, through the following always of the one upon the other of them. (219ᵃ14–19)

My suggestion is that the appeal to an analogy is different from the appeal to a relation of *following*. What explains the existence of a before and after in change is not the fact that change follows place. Instead, the explanation of the before and after in change appeals to an independent analogy that holds between change and place. This explanation, unlike those that invoke *following*, does not depend on the fact that each part of the change corresponds to a particular part of the change's path.[21]

The aim is to explain the asymmetry of the before and after in change by appealing to an analogy between the relations of positions on a line and the relations of stages in the change. The account, I suggest, is as follows. Consider a line ABC (with B before C on the line relative to the origin A) and a change that has stages P and Q. (This change need not be a movement over the line.)

---

[21] It does not depend, for instance, on the fact that each part of a spatial movement is over part of the movement's path or on the fact that any part of the path is the path of part of the movement. See Chapter 3, p. 49, for a discussion of the way in which explanations that invoke *following* depend upon such correspondences.

(i) The relation in which B stands to C on the line relative to the origin A is analogous to the relation in which one of the stages P and Q stands to the other.

(ii) P will be before Q in the change just in case it is *the relation in which P stands to Q* (rather than the relation in which Q stands to P) that is analogous to the relation in which B stands to C relative to A.

The analogy lies in the fact that just as a part of the line can exist even without the longer part that contains it, so also some parts of the change can occur though (because of interference) the rest of the change does not. The idea is that interfering with a change (and thus preventing part of it from occurring) is analogous to destroying part of a line.

To understand this, it is helpful to recall some of the things I said earlier about the before and after in place and its relation to the before and after in nature and substance. We saw earlier that B is before C on a line relative to an origin A just in case AB can exist without AC but AC cannot exist without AB (or, in other words, just in case AB is before AC in nature and substance). The new claim about the before and after in change is that P is before Q in a change, just in case, where O is the beginning of the change, the change-part OP can occur without the change-part OQ but not vice versa.

In order to develop this into an explanation of the asymmetry of the before and after in change, we need to have some account of what it is to be the beginning of the change. The before and after in a change is not relative to an arbitrary 'beginning' in the way that the before and after in place is relative to an arbitrary origin. This difference between the before and after in change and the before and after in place is reflected in a disanalogy between destroying parts of a line and interrupting a change. We can destroy parts from either end of a line, leaving the remainder of the line. In contrast, only certain parts of a change are parts that might be left over when the change is interrupted. I shall argue that (in a finitely long change) the change-parts that might be left over in this way all share a common boundary at one end of the change. We can define the beginning of the change as the common boundary of these change-parts. This allows us to give a non-temporal account of the before and after in a finite change:

Within any finite change, there is a set of change-parts that could be produced by interference. These change-parts all share a common limit. This limit is the beginning of the change. Call it O. A stage P is before a stage Q in the change iff the change part OP can occur without the change-part OQ occurring, but OQ cannot occur without OP occurring. (The end of the change will be the stage that stands to no other stage in the relation of before in that change.)[22]

A crucial step in this account is the claim that the change-parts that might be left over when the change is interrupted all share a common boundary. It is this fact that makes it possible to define the start of a change without presupposing temporal order. But what can be said in defence of this claim? It might be thought that, on the contrary, there are two different ways to interfere with a change. Consider for instance, the movement which is Socrates' walking from A to C along the following line:

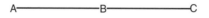

A————————B————————C

One way to interfere with this movement is to stop Socrates when he is part way through the movement, say when he is at B. This kind of interference does indeed leave a change-part that has a boundary at A. But is there not also a second type of interference? Surely, we could interfere with this movement by meeting Socrates in a car before he gets to A and driving him to some place, say B, in the path of the movement, leaving him to walk the rest of the way. If we did this, it seems, we would prevent the first part of the movement from occurring. What occurred would be a movement from B to C, and this movement would not have a boundary at A.

If I am right that there is a common boundary shared by all the change-parts that are left over when a change is interrupted, then there must be some principled way to discount this second type of interference. Aristotle would say, I think, that arranging matters so that Socrates never goes to A is not a way of interfering with a movement of his from A in such a way that only part of that movement is left. Rather, in

---

[22] It is important that on this account, the relation of P to Q in the change (when P is before Q in the change) is analogous *both* to the relation of point B to point C relative to the origin A *and* to the relation of B to A relative to the origin C (on the line A—B—C).

making him begin his movement from B, we are preventing *any* of his movement from A to C from occurring and bringing it about that a different movement occurs instead (a movement from B to C). When we interfere with an ongoing change, what is left is a part of the interrupted change. When we prevent a change from occurring and substitute a different change, the change that occurs (in this case the change from B to C) is not a remnant of the whole change (in this case, it is not a remnant of the change from A to C). The difference between these two cases is like the difference between erasing part of a line but leaving the remainder and erasing the whole of the line but drawing a shorter line in its place.

The reason for treating these two cases differently lies in Aristotle's account of change. It is essential to a change's being the change it is that it is a change from a particular state to a particular state (or, in the case of a movement, from a particular point to a particular point). As Aristotle says, just before the lines we are considering, a change is 'from something to something' (219ª10–11). The difference between the beginning and the end of the change is this. A changing thing can be going to a point C, even though it in fact never gets there. But a changing thing cannot be coming from a point A if it has never been there. This is because the potential governing a change is a potential to be in the terminus to which the changing thing is heading. When Socrates is moving from A to C a certain potential is actual in him, the potential to be at C. This potential is actual, if he is engaged in this change, regardless of whether he in fact ends up at C. We can, then, distinguish between the place in which a moving thing ends up and the place to which it was heading. There is no analogous distinction between where a thing is coming from and where it in fact started out. It follows that the only parts of a change that can occur without the whole change occurring are the parts that are bounded at one end by the beginning of the change.

INFINITELY LONG CHANGES

I have given an account of the before and after order in a *finite* change. There is an important class of changes to which this account does not apply. Aristotle thinks that certain changes have no beginning or end.[23] What, then, can he say about the before and after order of the stages in these changes?[24] The answer, I think, is that infinite changes do not exhibit the kind of asymmetrical before and after order that is found in finite changes. There is, of course, a series of stages in an infinite change, but for one of these stages to be before, rather than after, another is just for it to be temporally before.

This, at least, is a consequence of the account I have been attributing to Aristotle. But would he himself have accepted this consequence? Some remarks he makes at the end of *On Generation and Corruption* suggest that he might have done. He says there that the before and after order of stages in a finite change is asymmetrical in a way in which the before and after order of the stages in an infinite change is not. In the case of a finite change, such as the coming to be of a house, a later stage necessitates an earlier stage but not vice versa. If the house has come to be, it follows that the foundations have come to be, but the fact that the foundations have come to be does not guarantee that the house will come to be (since the process could be interrupted). Infinite changes, by

---

[23] Aristotle holds that the only infinitely long changes are circular movements. But it is the fact that these movements are infinitely long rather than the fact that they are circular that gives rise to the problem here. Though the before and after in place is not defined on a circular path, this does not imply anything about whether there can be a before and after relation in a circular change. The analogy that explains the before and after in a change makes no special reference to that change's path. It is an analogy between the change and *any* magnitude on which a relation of before and after in place can be defined.

[24] It might seem that my account could be modified so that it also applied to these changes. Instead of claiming that the parts that can be produced by interruption all share a common boundary, it would be necessary to claim that these parts are all infinite in one and the same direction (call this direction D). Let us use the label '−X' for a change-part that is bounded on one side by X and is infinite in this direction D. We could then say that a stage P is before a stage Q in an infinite change iff the change-part −P could occur without the change-part −Q but the change-part −Q could not occur without the change-part −P. There are two reasons why this account would be unsatisfactory. The first is that there would be no reason to think that all the change-parts that could be produced by interference must be infinite in one and the same direction. (Our reason for making the analogous assumption about finite changes relied upon the fact that the identity of such a change depended crucially on its being a change from a particular beginning towards an end.) The second reason is that on Aristotle's view, infinite changes are, by their very nature, impossible to interrupt. If the earlier stages of an infinite change occur, it is necessary that its later stages also occur (*Generation and Corruption* II.11.338ᵃ11–ᵇ5). There is, then, no sense in which a part of such a change (infinite in one direction but limited at a certain point P) might occur even though (because of interference) the whole change did not.

contrast, cannot be interrupted. For these changes, there is not the same asymmetry between the before and the after: if the later stage comes to be, then necessarily the earlier stage must have come to be and if the earlier stage comes to be, necessarily the later stage must come to be.[25]

IN WHAT SENSE IS THE BEFORE AND AFTER IN CHANGE *EXPLAINED* BY THE ANALOGY WITH THE BEFORE AND AFTER IN PLACE?

I have described the analogy between the before in place and the before in change and I have shown how this analogy can be used to give an account of the before and after in change. But in fact, Aristotle is claiming something more than that the analogy can be used in this way. He thinks that the before and after in place is primary and that it is the analogy with the before and after in place that explains the before and after in change.

Once again, then, we come up against the question of what justifies the claim about priority. In this case, the question is particularly pressing because relations of analogy are symmetrical: if X is analogous to Y then Y is analogous to X. In what sense, then, is the before and after in place primary? Why does the fact that it is analogous to the before and after in change imply that it should figure in the explanation of the before and after in change rather than vice versa?

Indeed, it might seem that on the account I have given, though the two kinds of before and after are analogous, each can be explained without any reference to the other. Whether or not one point is before another on a certain path relative to a certain origin depends on the relative distances of the two points from that origin. Whether one stage is before another in a change depends upon facts about whether certain parts of the change can or cannot occur without certain other parts. Why, then, does Aristotle not conclude that these two types of before and after are quite independent of each other?

The answer may just be that he is already committed to a pattern of explanation in which facts about spatial magnitude account for facts about change. He has already claimed that the continuity of magnitude

---

[25] *Generation and Corruption* II.11 (especially 338ª11–14).

explains the continuity of change. Once he has established that there is an analogy between the before and after in place and the before and after in change, it is, perhaps, natural for him to assume that in this case too the feature of magnitude explains the analogous feature of change.[26]

However, there is also an additional reason why Aristotle might have held that the before and after in place was explanatorily prior to the before and after in change. This is that the analogy between change and magnitude plays a role in the explanation of the before and after in change that it does not play in the explanation of the before and after in place. A crucial step in our account of the before and after in change was the claim that it is possible for part of a change to occur although, because of interference, the complete change does not. This claim presupposes that interrupting a change is, in a certain sense, analogous to destroying part of a line. When we destroy some of a line, what we are left with is part of the line. Initially, there existed a whole line, of which this was a part; when the rest of the line is destroyed, the part persists as a remnant. Describing what occurs when we interrupt a change is less straightforward. When the change is interrupted, the complete change never occurs. Because of this, it is not entirely obvious that what does occur can be regarded as a part. How can something be a part if there is never an existing whole of which it is a part?[27] In claiming that interrupting a change is analogous to destroying part of a line, Aristotle is

---

[26] This interpretation is supported by the fact that he introduces the claim that the before and after is first of all in place with the particle '*dē*' (which I have translated 'therefore', see above p. 47, footnote 2) and that he makes this claim just after his remarks about continuity.

[27] Change and magnitude differ in this way because the parts of a magnitude, unlike the parts of a change, persist. Aristotle is drawing attention to the fact that the parts of a spatial path persist, when he points out that the before and after in place is 'in position (*thesei*)' ($219^a15–16$). What he means by the expression 'in position' is explained by a passage in the *Categories* ($6.5^a15–37$). In this passage, he draws a contrast between those quantities the parts of which have 'position' in relation to one another and those quantities the parts of which do not have position in relation to one another. Examples of the former type of quantity are lines, planes, solids, and places. Examples of the latter are number, time, and (spoken) language. The distinction is this. Of the parts of a line, Aristotle says 'each of them is situated somewhere and you could distinguish them and say where each is situated in the plane and which one of the other parts it joins on to' ($5^a18–20$). By contrast, with language (and time) 'none of its parts persists, but once it has been said it can no longer be recaptured; so that its parts cannot have position, since none of them persists' ($5^a33–6$). It is because the parts of a change do not have 'position' (in this sense) that an account of the before and after in change needs to invoke the analogy between change and magnitude.

claiming that what is left when we interrupt a change should be regarded as a part of *the very change that would have occurred if there had been no interruption.*

For Aristotle, the need to appeal to the analogy here may be enough to show that the before and after in place is explanatorily prior to the before and after in change. On his view, we can only give an account of the before and after in change if we recognize that interrupting a change is analogous to destroying part of a line; there is no similar reason to appeal to this analogy in giving an account of the before and after in place.

TWO PROBLEMS FOR ARISTOTLE'S ACCOUNT

On the interpretation I have presented, Aristotle is attempting to explain temporal asymmetry by appealing to a more basic asymmetry that holds between the stages of individual changes. I shall end this chapter with two questions about this account.

The first question concerns the compatibility of the before and after series in different changes. Aristotle assumes that there is a single series of before and after in time and that this series follows all the before and afters in changes: if a stage P is before another stage Q in a change, then the time of P will be before the time of Q. But what justifies the assumption that there *can* be one temporal series that follows all these before and afters in changes? Why, in other words, is there any reason to think that these different before and after orders within changes will all be compatible with one another? On the account I have given, they are defined independently of one another. What, then, is to prevent its turning out that P is before Q in one change, R is before S in another change, but that P is simultaneous with S and Q is simultaneous with R?

It is interesting that Aristotle himself never raises this question.[28] Admittedly, in our passage he is focusing on the relation between a particular change and the time of that change, but one might expect

---

[28] Aristotle would presumably have thought that this question raised a serious problem. He assumes that the before and afters in changes must be compatible with each other. However, from our point of view, the possibility that these before and afters could be differently oriented does have one interesting and slightly surprising consequence. It suggests that there could be an Aristotelian account of a kind of time travel! Suppose that the changes that take place in *me* are all oriented in the opposite direction to

him to discuss this question about the compatibility of different changes at some later point. Perhaps the fact that he does not, tells us something about his aims here. On his view, there can only be an asymmetrical before and after in time because there are asymmetrical before and afters within changes. But he never claims that it is possible to give a *complete* explanation of the temporal before and after. This suggests that he is not engaged in an attempt to *reduce* temporal order to some other, more basic kind of order.

My second question is about the linearity of time. Aristotle presents an argument that time has no beginning or end,[29] but this, of course, leaves open the possibility that time might be circular. The closest he comes to considering this possibility is to argue that one and the same now cannot be both the beginning and the end of the same period of time. His argument that this is impossible is that opposites cannot 'hold simultaneously in respect of the same thing' ($222^{b}4$–6). As an argument against the view that time is circular, this simply begs the question. If time were circular, then *being temporally before a certain now* and *being temporally after that now* would not be opposites.[30]

the rest of the changes in the world. On Aristotle's view, the before and after in time follows the before and afters in changes. So if there are these two different incompatible orders of before and after in change, it looks as if there must be two differently oriented before and afters in time: one that follows the changes in me and another that follows all the other changes. This would provide Aristotle with the means to give an account of time travel very similar to the account that has been given, in our own day, by David Lewis. The idea that there could be two temporal before-and-afters that were differently oriented in the way I have described is, in fact, very like Lewis's idea that the order of certain events in what he calls 'personal time' might be different from their order in 'external time' (Lewis 1976).

[29] He gives two arguments. One argument starts from the claim that there has always been change ($222^{a}30$), a claim that is supported by the assumption that any beginning of change would have to have been triggered by some earlier change. (He argues most fully for this in *Physics* VIII.1.$251^{a}8$–$^{b}10$.) From this, he concludes that there must always have been time. The other argument rests on Aristotle's views about the now. Since any now is both a beginning and an end of time, there will be no first now (and, presumably, also no last now) ($222^{a}33$–$^{b}7$). Compare *Physics* VIII.1. $251^{b}19$–26, where he argues against Plato's view in the *Timaeus* that time was created.

[30] Aristotle characterizes the view he is attacking here as the view that there can be one and the same time repeatedly (*pollakis*) ($222^{a}30$–1). This suggests that he doesn't fully grasp what it might mean to claim that time is circular. Someone who holds that time is circular is not thereby committed to the view that one and the same time happens many times over.

In fact, the account I have attributed to Aristotle makes it particularly difficult for him to justify the assumption that time is linear. He cannot appeal to the structure of infinitely long changes, since they do not have an asymmetrical structure that is independent of time. He may simply be taking it for granted that time is linear. However, he does make some remarks elsewhere that could be developed into a defence of this assumption.

At the end of *On Generation and Corruption*, he says that there are certain infinitely long series of finite changes.[31] These are the series of the generations of a species of living thing. Such changes form a kind of cycle that goes on forever, but they differ in an important way from the cyclical changes of the planets. When a planet moves, there is one changing thing that is undergoing a repeated cyclical change (as Aristotle says, what recurs is 'the same in number'). Perishable things, by contrast, recur only 'in species' (338^b11–17). For example: 'Men and animals do not return upon themselves in such a way that the same individual comes to be again (for it is not necessary that if your father comes to be, you come to be, but it is necessary that if you come to be, he does)' (338^b8–11).

In such cases, then, there is a series of changes (the growth of this man, the growth of his father, the growth of his father's father, etc.), each of which is the same in kind as the last. All the changes in such a series are finite changes, so they each have their own asymmetrical before and after order. But as Aristotle himself remarks, there is also a kind of pretemporal before and after order that holds *between* the different changes in such a cycle: your coming to be presupposes your father's coming to be, but his coming to be does not presuppose yours (338^b9–11). A series of this sort forms a pretemporal order that is both infinite and (in the relevant sense) linear. Aristotle does not refer to this pretemporal order in his account of time, but it is interesting to note that by making this order part of the basis for the temporal before and after, he could have defended his assumption about time's linearity.

[31] *Generation and Corruption* II.11.

PART III

TIME AS A NUMBER
AND TIME AS A MEASURE

5

The Definition of Time as a
Kind of Number

Aristotle defines time as a kind of number. It is 'a number of change with respect to the before and after' ($219^{b}1$–2). He introduces this definition as if it is quite uncontroversial. He simply says, 'for this is what time is...' ($219^{b}1$). Though he goes on to explain the sense in which time is a kind of number, he does not really give us an argument for defining it in this way. He seems to think that the definition follows naturally from what he has already said. This suggests that if we want to understand the definition, it will be helpful to look at the passage that leads up to it.

In this passage, Aristotle has been explaining how it is that we mark the before and after in change:

We mark off these [the before and after in change] by taking them to be different from each other and some third thing between them. For whenever we think of the extremes as different from the middle and the soul says that the nows are two, one before and one after, then it is and this it is that we say time is. For that which is marked off by the now is thought to be time. Let us take this as true. ($219^{a}25$–30)

To mark the before and after in a change is to mark potential divisions in the change. These potential divisions are themselves indivisible. That is why there must always be 'some third thing in between them'. Aristotle's claim is that by marking these potential divisions in a change, we also mark two nows. Time is what is between two nows. 'That which is marked off by the now is thought to be time. Let us take this as true' ($219^{a}29$–30).

In defining time as a number of change, Aristotle is defining it as something that can be counted. The claim that time is 'marked off by the now' sheds some light on what he means by this. His view, I shall argue, is that we count time by counting nows. He introduces the idea that we count nows with his remark that we think there has been time whenever 'the soul says that the nows are two' (219ᵃ27–8). But it is only later that he explains how this bears on the way in which time is a number. He says (somewhat cryptically) that time is a number 'in the way that the extremes of a line are, and not in the way that the parts are' (220ᵃ16–17). Since he does not hold that time (any more than a line) is simply a collection of 'extremes' or limits, his thought must be that we count the parts of time by counting the nows that limit them (as we might count the parts of a line by counting the points that limit them). Again, he twice says that time's relation to a now is like a number's relation to a unit (220ᵃ4, 221ᵃ13–15). He is not claiming that time is a plurality of nows (as a number is a plurality of units), for he thinks that time is continuous. The sense in which a now is like a unit is that we count time by counting nows.[1]

When we count a now, we make a potential division in time. In doing so, we also make (and count) a potential division in any change that is then occurring.[2] Time is essentially a kind of *number* because it is, by definition, something that gets counted when we count the series of nows that Aristotle calls 'the before and after in time'. It is a number *of change with respect to the before and after* because in counting this series of nows we also count all changes, and we do so in such a way as to reflect the before and after orders within each of them.[3] To define time as something that is counted in this way is to define it as something that is essentially ordered. Time is a universal order within which all changes are related.

That, in brief, is Aristotle's view. But to understand it fully, we need to think more about what he means by 'the now' and by 'number'. I discuss

---

[1] He also makes the surprising claim that the now, in so far as it is something that counts, is itself a kind of number (at 220ᵃ22). The sense in which the now 'counts' is, I think, that we count time (and change) by counting the now.

[2] I explain this more fully in Ch. 7, below.

[3] Aristotle's view must be that we count the before and after in time by counting nows in accordance with the following rule: *For any two nows M and N, assign a lower number to M than to N if there is some change that has a stage* x *at M and a stage* y *at N and* x *is before* y *in that change. M is before N in time iff M is assigned a lower number than N.* In the last chapter, I asked whether Aristotle can defend his assumption that there *is* a series of nows that is infinite and linearly ordered and that reflects all the before and after relations within changes.

his account of the now in Chapters 7 and 8. In this chapter, I focus on his use of the notion of number. In what sense is time a kind of number? What is gained by talking of *counting* earlier and later times and nows as opposed to simply *marking* them?

The association between time and number goes back, at least, to Plato. In the *Timaeus*, we are told that the planets were brought into being to stand guard over the 'numbers of time' (38c). There the point seems to be that the planets, with their regular motions, mark out the units with which we measure time. Indeed, according to the *Timaeus*, time is *essentially* measurable: before the heavens came to be, there was no time, since there were 'no days or nights, no months or years' (37e).

Given this Platonic background, it is natural to suppose that Aristotle too thinks of time as something that is essentially measurable and that this is what he means when he defines it as a kind of number. After all, if we count nows that are separated by equal intervals, then our counting will enable us to measure both time and change. If, for example, I count a now whenever the big hand of my watch points to the numeral '12', then I am measuring out intervals of an hour. A change that starts when I count one of these nows and ends when I count the next must be exactly an hour long.

However, I shall argue that in defining time as a kind of number, Aristotle does not mean to define it either as a measure or as something measurable. His use of the word 'number' (*arithmos*) rather than 'measure' (*metron*) in this context is deliberate. I shall later defend this claim at length,[4] but it is worth mentioning here one argument in its favour. In the passage in which he introduces his definition, Aristotle says nothing about the need for the nows that we count to be at equal intervals from each other. If he were writing about *measurement*, then the intervals between the nows that were counted would be all-important. But he focuses instead on the *order* in which we count nows: on the fact that we count 'one before and one after' (219ª28).[5]

---

[4] See below pp. 96–8 and Ch. 6.

[5] It is important not to confuse order (in the sense of serial before and after order) with orderliness. On Plato's view, for there to be time, changes must be orderly. If time is to measure change, some changes have to have parts that are regularly repeated (so that there is a unit for counting). But being orderly is not the same as having a before and after order.

If I am right that Aristotle is distinguishing the claim that time is a number from the claim that it is a measure, his definition faces two obvious (and related) challenges. First, as we have seen, he thinks that time is continuous, but (at least, according to his standard view) only something that is a discrete collection of things can be a number (as opposed to a measurable magnitude). A number, he says, is a 'plurality of units'.[6] In the *Categories*, number is one of his main examples of a kind of quantity that is discrete: 'the parts of a number have no common boundary at which they join together' (*Categories* 6, 4ᵇ25–6).[7] How, then, can time possibly be a kind of number?[8]

The other challenge is to explain the sense in which we count nows. Again, the problem arises because time is continuous. As I have already said, Aristotle thinks that nows are potential divisions in time and that there can only be such potential divisions, in so far as we create them.[9] It follows that in counting nows, we are also bringing them into being. Moreover, since time is infinitely divisible, we can create indefinitely many potential divisions in it. Between any two nows that we count, we could always have counted another. But in that case, what is it to *count* nows? Counting, as it is normally understood, is a way of finding out how many things of a certain kind there are in a plurality. But how many nows there are itself depends on our counting: there will, necessarily, be just as many nows as we count. In this context, the notion of *counting* might seem to be devoid of any content.

If we are to understand how Aristotle would answer these two challenges, we need to look more closely at what he means by 'number' here. I shall argue that he holds that there is an extended sense of 'number' (a sense that is nonetheless distinct from *measure*) in which something continuous can be a number. He distinguishes between two types of number: numbers with which we count and numbers that are countable.

---

[6] *Metaphysics* X.1, 1053ª30, *Physics* III.7, 207ᵇ7. In this he is simply going along with a view common at this time. See Heath (1921: i. 69–70).

[7] For example, dividing ten into two fives is not like dividing a ten-foot line into two five-foot lines. The units in the ten are already separate from each other, so in dividing the ten, we do not need to create a new boundary, whereas when we divide a ten-foot line into two halves, we must separate what was originally joined together.

[8] This thought led ancient commentators, such as Strato and Plotinus, to argue that Aristotle would have done better to define time as a measure. Strato's view is reported by Simplicius, *In Phys.* 789, 2–4. Plotinus makes this objection in *Enneads* III.7.9.1–2.

[9] See Introduction, pp. 12–13.

Time, he says, is a number of the second sort: it is countable, but it is not a number with which we count.[10] As such, it can be continuous. Having singled out the sense in which time is a number, we shall be in a better position to understand what might be meant by the claim that nows are *counted*. In what follows I shall first describe the notions of number and counting that I take Aristotle to be employing here, and then show how he appeals to these notions to explain certain central features of time.

NUMBER, CONTINUITY, AND ORDER: TIME IS NOT A NUMBER WITH WHICH WE COUNT

Aristotle draws the distinction between numbers with which we count and numbers that are counted or countable shortly after giving his definition. It is, I think, a distinction between those numbers that are *only* countable and those that are *both* countable and also of the kind we count with. When he says that 'numbers with which we count are different from numbers counted', he does not mean to deny that a number with which we count can also itself be counted. All numbers are countable,[11] but what it is to be a number with which we count is different from what it is to be a number that can be counted: being a number with which we count involves more than just being a number that can be counted. Time is *only* a number that is countable; it is not the kind of number with which we count.

When we count, we put the things we are counting into a one-to-one correspondence with a sequence of numerals. We can do this directly (for instance, we can count three dogs by setting up a one-to-one correspondence between the dogs and the numerals '1, 2, 3') or we can do it indirectly (for instance, we can count how many laps a runner runs by laying down a pebble each time he goes past and then counting the number of pebbles).

---

[10] There is a hint of this more extended sense of 'number' in Aristotle's discussion of the infinite (*Physics* III.5.204b7–8). He says at one point that there can be no infinite 'separated number'. What he means by 'separated number' here is not clear, but on one plausible interpretation his claim is that there can be no infinite discrete plurality: there cannot be infinitely many separated parts. An unseparated number, in that case, would be something continuous, like time or a line. (This is Hussey's interpretation of this passage. See Hussey (1993: 79–80).)

[11] Aristotle standardly thinks of numbers as countable pluralities (see above, n. 6).

The set of numerals, '1, 2, 3', and the collection of pebbles are each of them numbers with which we count. Each is a number (since each is a finite plurality that can itself be counted) and, in the examples above, each is used in counting. Of course, the way in which we use the pebbles in counting is rather different from the way in which we use the numerals.[12] What is important for our purposes, though, is that something can only be used in either of these ways if it can be put into one-to-one correspondence with the thing counted. Because of this, something can only be a number with which we count if it is a discrete plurality.

When Aristotle denies that time is a number with which we count, he is not merely denying that it is, like the set of numerals or the set of pebbles in the above examples, a number we in fact use in counting. His point is that it is not even a number of the same *kind* as these. It is not, like these, a discrete plurality. He is using the expression 'number with which we count' in a broad sense to pick out any number that is (in this respect) *of the same kind as* the numbers we use in counting.

The distinction between numbers with which we count and numbers that are only countable is thus a distinction between the kind of number that is a discrete plurality and another kind of number that is continuous. Though Aristotle often uses the word 'number' (*arithmos*) simply to mean 'finite, discrete plurality',[13] in explaining his definition of time he says that something continuous can also be a number of a sort. We cannot use a continuous thing to count with (since it does not have discrete parts), but something continuous can be *countable*: when we mark off and count potential divisions in a continuous thing, we

---

[12]   Counting with some pebbles necessarily involves counting the pebbles, but when we count with a sequence of numerals, we do not also have to count the numerals. In using the signs '1, 2, 3' as a set of numerals, we have to take them in a certain order. (It matters that they are in the order '1, 2, 3' rather than the order '2, 3, 1'.) Because of this, we only need to know what was the last numeral in the sequence to know how many objects have been counted.

[13]   See n. 6 above. In fact, certain modern scholars have claimed that this is the only thing that is ever meant by the word '*arithmos*' in ancient Greek. Klein argues that in Greek thought *arithmos* 'never means anything other than a definite number of definite things' (1968: 7). Pritchard (1995: 30) is more circumspect. He says that 'the fundamental meaning of *arithmos* is *finite collection of items*', but he too assumes that this is the meaning of the word '*arithmos*' as it occurs in Aristotle's definition of time. He argues that 'since time is an *arithmos*, it is a finite set of units (themselves changes)' (p. 72). I do not dispute the claim that Aristotle generally thinks of an *arithmos* as a finite collection of things, but I shall argue that in his definition of time he is deliberately using the word in a non-standard sense.

are also, in a sense, counting the thing itself. So time can be a kind of number (a number that is only countable) even though it is continuous.

I have claimed that in defining time as a kind of number, Aristotle is defining it as something that is essentially ordered. The fact that numbers (in the sense of finite pluralities) stand in a certain kind of before and after order is something he emphasizes elsewhere.[14] But what, on his view, is the connection between being ordered and being a number *of the kind that is only countable*?

To answer this, it is necessary to address the second of the two challenges that I mentioned above: the challenge to explain the sense in which we can be said to *count* nows. Counting is ordinarily a way of finding out *how many* something or others there are, but how many nows there are itself depends on our counting. Hence, the point of counting nows (and the times that they limit) cannot be to find out how many of them there are. I want to suggest that, when we count nows, what is important is another, usually secondary, feature of counting. When we count, we arrange the objects that we count in a sequence by assigning numerals to them in order.[15] If our aim is to find out *how many* things of a certain kind there are, the order in which we count them is insignificant. We can find out how many words there are on a page just as well by counting from right to left as vice versa. In counting *nows*, though, the order is all-important. It does not matter *how many* nows we count; what is important is that we count a series of nows in a certain definite order (an order that reflects the different before and after orders within changes). Time is, by definition, something that is counted by counting nows in this way. As such, it inherits its order from the order of the nows that are counted.

This, I think, is the point Aristotle is making when he defines time as a number that is only countable. The main evidence for this

---

[14] In the *Categories*, for instance, he illustrates one of the senses of 'before' by explaining the way in which one is before two and two is before three. The explanation is that one unit can exist without two units but two units cannot exist without one unit, and two units can exist without three units but three units cannot exist without two (*Categories* 12.14ᵃ30–5). And in other works, when he mentions his view that there can be no common genus of things that exhibit a before and after order (a view he inherits from the Academy), his primary example of this is the number series (*Nicomachean Ethics* I.6 1096ᵃ17–19, *Metaphysics* III.3. 999ᵃ6–9).

[15] If I count a runner's laps using pebbles (as in the example above), then though I do not assign numerals to the laps directly, I do assign numerals to the pebbles as I count them.

interpretation of his distinction between the two kinds of number lies in the use he makes of the distinction later in his account. He invokes the fact that time is a number of a certain special kind in two different places: first, in giving his explanation of how time can be continuous; and second, in making the claim that earlier and later times are different from one another because earlier and later nows are. As we shall see, my interpretation shows how his distinction between different kinds of number is relevant in both these contexts.

It is worth noting that the fact that Aristotle appeals to the distinction in these ways is a reason for preferring my interpretation to one influential alternative. The distinction between numbers with which we count and numbers that are counted has sometimes been interpreted as a distinction between abstract numbers (for example, the number three or the number four) and collections of particular things, like three sheep or four triangles.[16] On this alternative interpretation, when Aristotle says that time is not a number with which we count, his point is that time is a number *of change*, rather than an abstract number like three or four. Though this is a possible interpretation, it does not, I think, explain the role the distinction plays in Aristotle's discussion. He draws the distinction immediately after giving his definition and he refers back to it later in his account.[17] If his point is merely that time is not an abstract number, then it is a little odd that he lays such emphasis on it. After all, the claim that time is a number of change already implies that it is not an abstract number. On my interpretation, the distinction has an important function in his account. This will become clearer, if we look at the passages in which Aristotle appeals to it.

ARISTOTLE'S USE OF THIS DISTINCTION
LATER IN HIS ACCOUNT

Aristotle explains the sense in which a continuous thing can be a number in some remarks at the beginning of IV.12. He points out that since time is continuous, there is no smallest time, and he says that

---

[16] This, for instance, is Hussey's interpretation (1993: 151).

[17] Certainly, at 220^{b}8–10, and I shall argue that he is also invoking the same distinction at 220^{a}27–32 (though there he describes it as a distinction between number *simpliciter* and a number of another kind).

this might be thought to show that time is not a kind of number at all. Against such a view, he claims that there is a kind of number of which there is also no smallest.

The smallest number that is *simpliciter* is the two, but there is number *of a sort* of which in a way there is and in a way there is not a smallest. For instance, of the line the least in multiplicity is the two lines or the one, but in magnitude there is not a least. For every line is always divided. So similarly also for time. The smallest according to number is the one time or the two, but according to magnitude there is not a smallest.   (220ª27–32)

As we have already seen, Aristotle's standard view is that a number is a plurality of units. This suggests that 'a number which is *simpliciter*' is a number of this kind. He says that the smallest number of this kind is the two. In other words, the smallest *plurality* is a plurality of two things.[18] But, he says, there is also another kind of number. Continuous things, like lines, are countable. We can count them by dividing them. In that sense, they are numbers of a sort.

But though there is a way in which continuous things (like discrete pluralities) have a least, there is also a way in which they do not. The sense in which a line (considered as something countable) has 'a least' is this. If we mark out a line into parts and count the parts, there will be a least number of parts. Aristotle says that 'of the line, the least in multiplicity is the two lines or the one' (220ª28–9). (Two is the smallest plurality. If we count two *dividing-points* in the line we shall have counted one line-part, though strictly speaking the smallest number of *line-parts* is two.) The sense in which a line does not have 'a least' is that there is no smallest possible magnitude of a line. There is thus no limit to the smallness of the parts we mark. Between any two divisions, we could always make another one. (That is just what it is for a line to be continuous, in Aristotle's sense.)

---

[18] This view that two is the smallest number is also found elsewhere. At *Phaedo* 104a–b, Plato lists the odd numbers as 3, 5, ... At *Parmenides* 144a, he argues that if one is, there must *also* be number. Euclid says that the unit is that in virtue of which each of the things that exist is called one and number is a multitude made up of units (*Elements* VII defn 1 and 2).

The same is true of time. Time is a kind of number because we can count it by making potential divisions in it.[19] There is, in a sense, a least number of times that can be marked out in this way. (Again, Aristotle says that this least number is the one or the two: by making two potential divisions, we mark out one period of time, but the smallest plurality of periods of time is two periods.) But there is no least time: however small a period of time we mark out, we could always have marked out a smaller one.

Aristotle appeals once again to the fact that time is a number of this peculiar kind, when he is explaining why earlier and later times are different:

Time is not a number with which we count but the number that is counted, and this turns out to be always different before and after, because the nows are different. The number of a hundred horses and of a hundred men is one and the same, but the things of which it is a number are different—the horses are different from the men.   (220^{b}8–12)

He makes two distinct claims in this passage. He claims that earlier and later nows are different. And he also claims that it is because earlier and later nows are different that earlier and later times are different. It is important to be clear which of his remarks is relevant to which claim. I shall argue that he supports the former claim by comparing nows to different collections of a hundred, and he supports the latter claim by reminding us that time is a number counted, not a number with which we count.

The remark about the hundred men and horses is meant to explain the fact that earlier and later nows are different. We count change-stages by counting the nows that bound them. The nows differ from each other because they bound different collections of changes. Just as a hundred horses is different from a hundred men (though both are hundreds), so also the now that divides the set of changes that are going on at six o'clock will be different from the now that divides the set of changes that are going on at seven o'clock (though they are

---

[19] In this sense, of course, a line too is a kind of number. Time is more closely associated with number than is a line, as time is defined as a kind of number. But this difference is not relevant here, where we are merely trying to show how it is possible for time to be (either essentially or accidentally) a kind of number.

both nows).[20] The hundred horses differs from the hundred men because the horses differ from the men. The now at six o'clock differs from the now at seven o'clock because the changes going on at six o'clock differ from the changes going on at seven o'clock.

It is in the course of defending his other claim (that because earlier and later nows are different, earlier and later times are different too) that Aristotle reminds us that time is a number counted rather than a number with which we count. Since time is not the kind of number that is a discrete plurality, it is something that can only be counted by being marked out. As we have seen, time is marked out by nows. This is why the sameness and difference of times depends on the sameness and difference of nows. Since earlier and later nows are always different, and time is the kind of number that must be marked out by such nows, earlier and later times are always different too.[21]

On the interpretation I have been presenting, Aristotle recognizes that time is only a number in a somewhat extended sense. The word '*arithmos*' is standardly used to refer to numbers with which we can count: 'numbers *simpliciter*'. But obviously, he does not simply mean to be using language in an idiosyncratic way. The point of calling time a kind of number is that it has something in common with numbers with which we count. Like them, it has a certain kind of before and after order. He needs, then, to show that the extension he proposes has some basis in the existing use of the word. The fact that time is countable provides some justification for calling it a number. He also points out that there are two further ways in which time is similar to what would normally be thought of as a number. First, like any number, time is said to be much and little (though, as it is continuous, it is also said to be long and short). Second, neither time nor a number with which we

---

[20] This suggests that there is some sense in which earlier and later nows are the same. (They are all nows, just as the hundred horses and the hundred men are both hundreds.) I discuss the sameness of earlier and later nows in Ch. 8, below. Aristotle's use of this comparison with numbers to explain the difference between earlier and later nows is puzzling, since he elsewhere uses a similar comparison to explain how there can be one and the same time of all simultaneous changes. I explain these comparisons more fully in Ch. 7, below.

[21] Obviously, different sets of nows can be used to divide up one and the same period of time. We might divide a particular hour by counting a now every five minutes or we might divide it by counting nows at irregular intervals. Aristotle's point must be that the identity of a period of time depends on the pair of nows that bounds it.

count is said to be fast or slow: 'It is not fast or slow—for nor is any number with which we count fast or slow' (220^{b}4–5). What are fast or slow are changes, not pluralities of things.[22] In this respect, time is like a discrete plurality or number with which we count, rather than like a change.[23]

AGAINST THE ALTERNATIVE VIEW THAT ARISTOTLE DEFINES TIME AS A MEASURE

In this chapter, I have discussed how Aristotle can make sense of the claim that time, though continuous, is nevertheless a kind of number. But, as I said earlier, his account is often interpreted in such a way that this question does not arise. It is often assumed that when he defines time as a number, he really just means that it is a measure. On this interpretation, there is no puzzle about how his definition of time is compatible with his claim that time is continuous.[24]

---

[22] *We* might want to object that we can speak of a plurality of *changes* as being fast or slow. For example, we might say: 'the plurality of all train journeys in France is faster than the plurality of all train journeys in England'. But, in so far as this claim makes sense to us, it is because we have the idea of average speed. What we mean is that the average speed of train journeys in France is greater than the average speed of train journeys in England. Aristotle, lacking any such notion, would have denied that a plurality of changes can be said to be fast. What are fast or slow are individual changes.

[23] Annas (1975: 97, n. 3) claims that in this passage Aristotle is treating time as a number with which we count. This shows, she thinks, that he does not stick consistently to the distinction between the two types of number. My interpretation shows that we need not accuse him of inconsistency here.

[24] Many commentators claim that Aristotle defines time either as a *measure of change* or as *what is measured in change*. Moreau (1965: 129–30) calls time 'the measurable aspect of change'; Zeller (1878: ii. 299) says that 'it is the measure or the number'; Hussey (1993: p. xxxviii) claims that when Aristotle defines time as a number of change, his 'thought is that (roughly) there is nothing more to time than that it is a measurable quantity which attaches to changes in just the same sort of way as e.g. length and heaviness attach to material bodies'; Julia Annas (1975: 97–113) argues that in these chapters of the *Physics*, Aristotle is not distinguishing between number and measure. Destrée (1991), Conen (1964), Seeck (1987), and Sorabji (1983) are the only interpreters I have found who argue that Aristotle is distinguishing here between number and measure.

Aristotle does say, later in his account, that time is a kind of measure of change.[25] I discuss what he means by this in the next chapter. But the suggestion that he is *defining* time as a kind of measure is implausible. The remarks he makes when he presents the definition give us no reason to think that the point he is making here is about measurement rather than counting. For one thing, as I mentioned earlier, he says nothing in this passage about the need to find some unit for measuring change. When we measure the duration of a change, we have to fix upon some way of marking out equal intervals. We need, that is, to find some regularly repeated change to use as a kind of clock. As we have already seen, the definition of time is presented as the conclusion of an account of the circumstances under which we are aware that time has passed. Aristotle never suggests that we will only know that time has passed if we are able to refer to some periodic change. Instead, he says that we know time has passed whenever we distinguish between two different 'nows' or instants (219ᵃ26–9). These arguments are clearly intended to support the claim that time is what we count by counting nows. They are not designed to show that time is something by which we *measure* change.

The only explicit mention of measurement in *Physics* IV.11 is in a discussion of the now. He says that the now measures change by being before and after (219ᵇ11–12). But although he uses the word 'measure' here, the idea that the now *measures* change is puzzling on any view.[26] Perhaps his point is that the now's dividing changes into before and after stages is one of the preconditions for measuring change.

He makes only one other remark that might suggest he is concerned with measurement here. Just after giving the definition, he says that the fact that we judge the quantity of time by means of change is a sign that time is a kind of number: 'we judge the greater and less by number, and the greater and less change by time' (219ᵇ3–5). However, nothing forces us to take this as a remark about measurement. The process of counting nows itself provides a way of comparing the lengths of some changes. For example, whether or not the intervals between the nows counted are

[25] For example, he says this at IV.12.220ᵇ14–16.

[26] For this reason, Ross, in the Oxford Classical Text, emends 'measures' (*metrei*) to 'bounds' (*horizei*), but all the manuscripts except one (E) have '*metrei*', and this was the reading of all the Greek commentators.

equal, if two changes begin at the same now, then we know that the longer of them is the one that ends at the later now.[27]

I have argued against the view that Aristotle means to define time as a measure of change. Those who put forward this view sometimes claim that he uses the words 'number' and 'measure' interchangeably.[28] To see what is wrong with this claim, it is necessary to look more generally at his account of the relation between number and measure. It is to this that I now turn.

---

[27] Even if we do take Aristotle to be referring to time's use as a measure of change here, this does not show that when he calls time a number he means that it is a measure. The fact that time is used to measure change would still only be cited as a sign (*sēmeion*) that time is a kind of number.

[28] Annas (1975: 98–100).

6

Time as a Measure of Change

Aristotle does not *define* time either as a measure or as something measurable, but he holds nevertheless that it is both: it measures change and it is measured by change. What, then, is the relation between his definition of time as something countable and his claim that it is measurable? And what does he mean when he says that change is measured by time?

THE RELATION BETWEEN COUNTING
AND MEASURING

Aristotle writes frequently of 'measuring' a number. In IV.12, he says that 'by the one horse we measure the number of horses' (220^b19–20). In the *Metaphysics*, he describes number as 'a plurality measurable by one' (*Metaphysics* X.6, 1057^a3–4) and as 'a measured plurality and plurality of measures' (*Metaphysics* XIV.1, 1088^a5–6). This has led some commentators to claim that he equates number and measure, and that he writes indiscriminately of 'counting' and 'measuring' when he means *finding the quantity of* something.[1]

I have already argued that the word 'number', as it occurs in his definition of time, has a special sense. To define time as something countable is to say that it is essentially ordered, rather than that it is essentially a kind of quantity. From this, it follows that the claim that time is a number of change is quite distinct from the claim that it is a measure of change. Counting the before and after in time is a way of ordering changes; it is not in itself a way of finding out how much

---

[1] See, for example, Julia Annas (1975: 98).

change has passed. If this is right, then Aristotle's definition of time is one instance in which he is not equating counting and measuring.

In this chapter, however, my interest is primarily in the remarks he makes about time and measurement. To understand these, it is necessary to get clearer about the relation between measuring and the ordinary kind of counting: the kind of counting we use to find the quantity of something. I argue that Aristotle does not equate measuring even with this kind of counting. Instead, he treats this kind of counting as a special *type* of measuring. It is the type of measuring we use to find the quantity of a discrete collection of things, but it cannot be used to find the quantity of something continuous. To find the quantity of a continuous thing, we must use another type of measuring: weighing, for instance, (if we want to find out how heavy something is) or measuring with a ruler (if we want to find out how long something is). On Aristotle's view, counting (even when it is a means of finding the quantity of something) is importantly different from these types of measuring. As a means of finding the quantity of something, counting is 'exact' in a way that other types of measuring cannot be. Aristotle says that the types of measuring that we use to find the quantity of a continuous magnitude 'imitate' the exactness of counting.

This is why, though it is not surprising to find Aristotle writing of 'measuring' a number (using the more generic word 'measuring', where he could have used the more specific, 'counting'), it calls for some special explanation, when he writes of counting, or finding the number of, something continuous, like time. Strictly speaking, we cannot find out how much there is of some continuous thing by counting it; we must use instead some other, less exact type of measurement. Here, then, we have an independent argument for the conclusion I reached in the last chapter. When he defines time as something countable, Aristotle means 'countable' to be understood in a special sense: to define time as something countable is not to define it as something quantifiable.

This, I shall argue, is Aristotle's view of the relation between counting (when it is a way of finding the quantity of something) and measuring. Obviously, the brief outline I have given above leaves much unexplained. In what sense is counting more exact than other types of measuring? And what does it mean to claim that these other types of measuring 'imitate' counting? Answers to these questions can be found in his more general discussion of number in *Metaphysics* X.[2] In what follows, I shall first look at this more general discussion and then go on to explain its relevance to Aristotle's claims in the *Physics* about the measurement of time and change.

COUNTING AND MEASURING IN *METAPHYSICS* X

Though he does not equate counting and measuring, Aristotle does think that there is a way in which counting a collection of things is *like* measuring a continuous magnitude. Counting, like the measurement of something continuous, involves a choice of unit. Before we can count, we need to know what we are counting: are we counting men or battalions? Before we can measure, we need to know what we are measuring: are we measuring with a unit of length or with a unit of weight?[3] In each case, the unit must be of the same kind as the thing measured or counted. For instance, the unit used to measure a length must be a length and the unit used to measure a weight must be a weight. We cannot measure lengths in pounds or weights in inches:

The measure is always cogeneric (*suggenes*) [with the thing measured]; the measure of spatial magnitudes is a spatial magnitude, and in particular that of length is a length, that of breadth is a breadth, that of voiced sound a voiced

---

[2] Annas (1975: 98) invokes this discussion in support of her view that Aristotle equates number and measure.

[3] It is important, I think, that it is *this* choice of unit for measuring that Aristotle has in mind. There are, in fact, two choices of unit that we must make before we start to measure. Suppose I am going to measure a table. I must first decide whether I am going to measure it with a unit of length or a unit of weight. That is, in a sense, I must decide *what* quantity I am going to measure: am I going to weigh the table or find out how long it is? After this there is a second choice to be made. I must decide *which* unit of length or unit of weight I am going to use. Shall I measure in inches or in centimetres, in pounds or in kilos? Julia Annas (1975: 99–100 and 1976: 36–7) does not draw a distinction between these two choices of unit, but her comments suggest that she thinks Aristotle is comparing the choice between counting men and counting battalions to the kind of choice we make when we decide whether to measure in inches or in centimetres. This is, indeed, one of her reasons for thinking that Aristotle equates counting and measuring. It will be important to bear in mind that this is *not* the comparison that he is making, if we are to understand his claim that counting is more exact than other types of measuring.

sound, that of weight a weight, that of units a unit. (*Metaphysics*, X.1.1053ᵃ24–7)⁴

Similarly, if we are going to count colours, our unit will not be the abstract *one*; it will, rather, be one *colour*. If we are going to count tunes, our unit will be one quarter-tone:

> If the things that are were colours, the things that are would have been a number, but of what? Clearly of colours; and the one would have been a particular one, e.g. white. And similarly if the things that are were tunes, they would have been a number, but a number of quarter-tones.... And the same account applies to other genera.... In all cases the number is a number of somethings, and the one is one something. (*Metaphysics*, X.2.1053ᵇ32–54ᵃ7)

When we choose whether to measure in units of weight or in units of length, this is a choice about what is to be measured (weight or length) just as when we choose whether to count horses or men, this is a choice about what is to be counted. In both cases, the unit we choose must be of the same type, or genus, as the thing we are measuring or counting.

This is the way in which counting a collection of things is similar to measuring something continuous. But there are also two important respects in which counting is different. First, once we have chosen the unit for counting, we only have to count how many of those units there are in a collection to find out its number. But after choosing to measure with a unit of length or a unit of weight, there is still a further choice to be made. We still have to decide how big a unit to use: whether to measure in inches or in centimetres, whether to measure in pounds or in kilograms.

The other way in which counting a collection differs from measuring a continuous quantity is this. When we count a collection of things, we find out (if we count correctly) exactly how many things there are in the collection. But when we count the centimetre-long parts of a line, this does not tell us the exact length of the line. The reason for this is that the unit we use for measuring may not fit an exact number of times along the thing to be measured.⁵ *We* would avoid any inexactness here by

---

⁴ It is puzzling that Aristotle lists length and breadth here as requiring two different types of measure. I am not sure what to say about this.

⁵ Even in cases when the unit does in fact fit an exact number of times, counting the number of times does not tell us the exact length of the line. To know that the number of times the centimetre unit fits along the measured line is *ten* is not yet to know whether or not it fits exactly ten times.

using fractions (or, where the length to be measured was incommensurable with the unit chosen, irrational numbers), but Aristotle does not regard fractions or irrationals as numbers. On his view, neither a fraction nor an irrational number can be an appropriate answer to a *how many* question. For example, 'half a foot' cannot be an appropriate answer to the question 'how many feet is this?' A length of one and a half feet can be accurately measured using a unit that is half a foot long (it will be three half-feet), but it cannot be accurately measured in feet.

This explains why Aristotle thinks that measurement is 'less exact' than counting. There is, he points out, a way to minimize this inexactness. The smaller the unit we choose, the more exact our measurement will be. Because of this, for each type of quantity measured, there is a preferred unit of measurement. This is the smallest perceivable unit, the unit that is 'indivisible in relation to perception'. When we count, we use indivisible units, units from which it is impossible to 'take away or add' (even when the units are ordinary things like horses or men, they are treated as indivisible for the purposes of counting). If our measuring is to approximate as closely as possible to the exactness of counting, then we should use units for measuring that are as like indivisible units as possible. The units we choose should be the smallest practicable:

For from the stade or talent or anything relatively large something added or taken away might more escape notice than from something smaller; so that the first thing from which, as far as perception goes, this is not possible, everyone makes the measure, whether of liquids or of solids, whether of weight or of size; and they think they know the quantity when they know it through this measure. (*Metaphysics*, X.1.1053ª2–8)

Given this view of measuring, if we are measuring a continuous quantity, then however small a unit we choose, measurements using that unit will, in many cases, be inexact. Even very small units may not fit perfectly into the thing to be measured. These types of measuring cannot, then, match the exactness of counting. They are the best imitations of counting that we can have when we are dealing with continuous quantities:

Where it is thought impossible to take away or to add, this measure is exact (therefore that of number is most exact; for they posit the unit as indivisible in every way); and in all other cases they imitate something of this sort. (*Metaphysics*, X.1.1052ᵇ35–53ª2)

We have seen that Aristotle does not equate counting and measuring. To find the quantity of something that is continuous, we must use a method of measurement that is less exact than counting. Hence, if he says that we 'count' something continuous, he is either using the word 'count' in a loose sense (when he should, strictly speaking, have said 'measure') or he is using it to mean something other than *find the quantity of.*

It is, of course, not impossible that he should be using this word loosely in his discussion of time in the *Physics*. Indeed, there is one place where he writes 'counted' but clearly means measured. This is a passage in which he is pointing out one of the similarities between counting and other types of measuring. Everything, he says 'is counted by some one thing of the same type, units by a unit, horses by a horse and thus also time by a certain definite time' (223^{b}13–15). His point here must be that we *measure* time using some unit of time. However, it is, I think, unlikely that he would use the notions of number and counting in this loose way in his definition of time. This definition has a central role in his whole discussion. As we have seen, he goes to some lengths to explain in exactly what sense time is a countable number, and he invokes the fact that it is a number of this sort to explain several aspects of its nature. Here, if anywhere, one would expect him to choose his words carefully. It is safe to assume, then, that in the context of the definition 'counted' does not mean measured. To define time as something countable is not (for Aristotle) to define it as something measurable. He defines time as a kind of order, not as a kind of quantity.

Aristotle's views about the units that should be used for measurement also have a more direct bearing on his account of time. As we have seen, he thinks that the unit used for measuring (or indeed, for counting) must be of the same type as the thing that is to be measured (or counted). And he holds that when measuring a continuous magnitude, a unit should be chosen that is of the smallest size practicable. Both of these views lie behind his remarks in the *Physics* about the measurement of time and of change.

THE CLAIM THAT WE MEASURE CHANGE BY TIME AND TIME BY CHANGE

Though he does not define time as something measurable, Aristotle does claim that we measure change by time and time by change. He sets himself to explain how this is possible.[6] There are, he seems to think, two things that call for explanation, both of them concerning the unit for measurement. First, since earlier and later times and changes are always different, we cannot directly compare the lengths of two non-simultaneous times or changes (as we might, for instance, compare two spatial magnitudes by setting them next to each other). How, then, are we to determine that earlier and later units of time are all of the same magnitude? Second, as we have already seen, a unit must be of the same kind as the thing it measures (or so, at least, Aristotle assumes). If time is to measure change, or vice versa, then time and change must be, in the relevant sense, of the same kind. But what justification is there for assuming that they are, in fact, of the same kind?

He addresses the first of these questions in chapter 14 ($223^{b}12$–$224^{a}2$). If we are to measure change, we need to mark out nows that are equidistant from each other. To do this we need some repeated change to serve as a standard. The change that serves this purpose is the uniform circular motion of the outermost sphere.[7]

Aristotle has two reasons for thinking that the movement of the outermost sphere is the primary measure of time. The first is that this movement is a rotary motion. Rotary movements are, on Aristotle's view, the only movements that can go on forever. They are also, he claims, the only natural movements that are regular.[8] It follows that if

---

[6] *Physics* IV 12.$220^{b}14$–32 and 14.$223^{b}12$–$224^{a}2$.

[7] Because of this, time *qua measure* is tied to a particular movement in a way in which time *simpliciter* cannot be. This brings out a distinction between time's use as a number and time's use as a measure. When Aristotle introduces his definition of time, he implies that we can count change by counting divisions in *any* changes ($219^{a}22$–9). He emphasizes this point again in chapter 14, saying that time is a number of continuous change in general, not just a number of some particular change ($223^{a}33$–$^{b}1$). But there are only certain particular changes—regular changes—by means of which we can make temporal measurements. Some commentators have concluded, because of this, that time is the number only of the movement of the outermost sphere. This, I think, is a consequence of confusing the claim that time is a number with the claim that it is a measure. Thus, Philoponos says: 'Time is not a number of all change (for it is not a number of alteration or growth) but rather of change in place, and not of every kind of change in place but of the orderly change. For time measures every change, but primarily the orderly change, through which it also measures the others. For day and season and month and year are measured by the period of the fixed [stars], and by means of this change time measures all change. So that it is of this kind of change that time is a number' (Philoponos *In Phys.* 718, 14–20).

[8] In our passage of *Physics* IV, he says that rotary motion is most of all a measure because the number (that is, the time) of this kind of motion is 'most knowable'. He goes on to explain that there is uniform motion, but not uniform qualitative change, growth

we count the revolutions of the outermost sphere, we shall be marking out equal intervals of time. Aristotle's second reason for making the movement of the outermost sphere the primary measure is that this is generally thought to be the fastest regular movement: 'they assume the movement of the heavens to be uniform and the quickest, and judge the others by reference to it' (*Metaphysics* X.1, 1053^a 10–12). He appeals here to his view, explained above, that quite generally, the smallest practicable unit is the most appropriate measure.[9] Just as we use a quarter-tone as a unit in music (since this is the least interval), so also we use the movement of the heavens as a unit for measuring change (since this is the quickest movement and hence 'occupies the least-time') (1053^{a}8–13). He holds, then, that the primary measure of time and change is the motion of the celestial sphere: 'other changes are measured by this one, and time is measured by this change' (223^{b}21–3).

The other question Aristotle needs to answer is how, if time is not a kind of change, it is possible for it to measure change or vice versa. Strictly speaking, his view is that what measures both time and change is a unit of change: 'time is measured by change and change by time; that is, the quantity of the change and of the time is measured by the change defined by the time' (223^{b}15–18). Time measures change 'by defining some change which will measure out the whole change' (221^{a}1–2). What is 'defined' here is really a change-part. It is defined by time in the sense that its beginning and end are marked out by nows. When marked out in this way, the change-part serves as a unit to measure both the quantity of the whole change and the quantity of the time.

This raises a puzzle. We have already seen that Aristotle thinks the unit with which we measure must be of the same kind as the thing measured. In this respect measuring something continuous is like counting a plurality of things.[10] As he puts it here: 'each thing is counted by some one thing of the same type, units by a unit, horses by a horse, and thus also time by a certain definite time' (223^{b}13–15).[11]

---

or coming to be (223^{b}18–21). His fullest discussion of rotary motion is in *Physics* VIII.7–9. He claims there that rectilinear movements, unlike rotary movements, always accelerate towards some goal (9.265^{b}11–16).

[9] See above, p. 103.

[10] See above, pp. 101–2.

[11] As I explained earlier, when he says here that time is 'counted' by some definite time, he must, I think, be speaking loosely. What he really means is that time is measured by some definite time. (See above, p. 104.)

The puzzle, then, is this. Given that time is not a kind of change, how can we use a unit of change to measure time?[12]

Aristotle answers this puzzle in chapter 12 when he asks how it is possible that we can measure time by change and change by time.[13] He provides two different answers. First, he appeals to the fact that time is a number of change:

Not only do we measure change by time but also time by change, because they are defined by one another. The time defines the change, being its number, and the change the time. (220^{b}14–18)

'Defines' here, must have the sense 'marks out'. Only in that sense does time define change. Aristotle is claiming that since we can divide change by dividing time and vice versa, time and change must be (in the relevant sense) of the same kind.

This shows that change and time are related in such a way that it is possible for one to measure the other. Aristotle adds that we measure both time and change using a unit change, just as we measure both a multiplicity of horses and a number of horses using a unit horse:

---

[12] Philoponos, in his commentary, explains the difficulty. (He concentrates on the question how time is the measure of change, rather than how a unit of change can be used to measure time. I think it is better to put the puzzle in this second way, because the sense in which time is the measure of change is that the unit of change, marked out by time, measures change.) Philoponos says: 'He inquires first how time is the measure of change. For it is reasonable to find a certain puzzle in this. The measure should be *homogenes* with the changing thing. For we measure number by the unit. We measure ten horses by the horse and wood by the piece of wood. So if time is not *homogenes* with change (for it has been shown that time is not change), how can we say that change is measured by time?' (Philoponos *In Phys.* 745, 31–746, 4.)

[13] I take this to be the puzzle: how is it possible for time to measure change or change to measure time, given that time is not a kind of change and change is not a kind of time? Alternatively, the puzzle he is raising here could be about reciprocity: how can it be the case both that X measures Y and that Y measures X? But I think this is unlikely to be something that Aristotle would find *prima facie* puzzling. On his view, it is quite generally true that when one thing measures another, what is measured can also be used as a measure. For example, if it is possible to weigh a pound of sugar with iron weights, then it is also possible to use the sugar to identify which combination of weights is equal to one pound. Moreover, part of Aristotle's solution to the puzzle is to say that time follows change. It is not clear how this could be a solution to the puzzle about reciprocity, as *following* is itself an asymmetrical relation.

for it is by the number that we come to know the multiplicity of horses, and conversely (*palin*), by the one horse that we come to know the number of horses itself. Similarly, in the case of time and change, we measure the change by the time and the time by the change.   (220^{b}20–4) [14]

His thought seems to be this. We use the one horse to measure both the 'multiplicity of horses' and also 'the number of horses itself'. In fact, to measure the multiplicity of horses is just to measure their number. Similarly, we use a unit of change to measure how long some changes are and also to measure their time (since to measure how long they are is just to measure their time). The way Aristotle makes this point is misleading. It suggests that the sense in which we know the multiplicity of horses 'by the number' is the same as the sense in which we know the number 'by the one horse'. [15] But this cannot be his view. The sense in which we come to know the number of horses 'by the one horse' is that we use the unit horse to help us find out how many horses there are: when we count, we apply our knowledge of what it is for something to be one horse. The sense in which we know the multiplicity of horses 'by number' is quite different: knowing the multiplicity of the horses (that is, knowing how many there are) *just is* knowing the number of horses. Our knowledge of the number is not something we use in finding out how many horses there are. [16] As we have seen, the relation between time

[14] We should not be surprised that in this passage, Aristotle uses the word 'measure' to describe the single horse's relation to the number of horses. As I explained above, Aristotle thinks that counting is an exact kind of measuring, so he does sometimes use the word 'measure' where we would expect him to say 'count'.

[15] This is suggested both by his repeated use of the dative (which I have been translating 'by') and by the contrast he draws between knowing the horses by the number and knowing the number by the one horse. That this is meant to be a contrast is implied by his use of the word *palin* (conversely) and of the construction *men ... de* (on the one hand ... on the other hand).

[16] There is an alternative way to interpret this passage, but this alternative interpretation leaves Aristotle with an equally unsatisfactory position. When he says that it is by the number that we come to know the multiplicity of the horses, he could mean that we come to know the multiplicity of horses by making use of numbers with which we count. We come to know the multiplicity of horses by setting up a one-to-one correspondence between the horses and the number with which we are counting (which could, for instance, be a sequence of numerals). But if this is what Aristotle is saying here, then he is equivocating between two senses of 'number'. The sense in which we use the unit horse to find out the number of horses is that we use the unit to find out *how many* horses there are. (In fact, we use both the unit horse and the number with which we count to find out how many horses there are.) We do not use the unit horse as a way of coming to know *the number with which we are counting* the horses. We use it, along with the number with which we are counting them, to arrive at an answer to the question 'how many?'.

and change is asymmetrical in the same way. We use a unit of change to measure both change and time.

Aristotle's other explanation of the fact that time and change can be used to measure each other appeals to the fact that time follows change. 'It is reasonable', he says, 'that this should turn out so, for change follows magnitude and time follows change, in being a quantity and continuous and divisible' (220^b24–6). Since time follows change, for any part of a change there is a corresponding part of the time of the change (and vice versa). Similarly, since change follows magnitude, for any part of a magnitude, there is a corresponding part of the movement over the magnitude (and vice versa). This guarantees that it is possible for time to measure change (and vice versa), and also that it is possible for movement to measure magnitude (and vice versa). As Aristotle says, 'we say the road is long if the journey is long, and we say the journey is long if the road is' (220^b29–31). In the same way, we can say that the change is long because its time is long and that the time is long because the change is.

Aristotle's account explains how time and change can be the sort of things that measure each other. This is possible, he says, because time follows change and is a number of change. But if time is to measure change or vice versa, it is not enough that time and change are related in these ways. There must also be some regular, repeated change that can serve as a clock. Aristotle never suggests that the existence of such a clock is essential to time. He defines time as a number of a certain special kind: a number that we count by counting nows. He does not define it as a kind of measure.[17]

[17] If my interpretation is right, then it undermines an objection that Gregory Vlastos has made to Aristotle's account of time. Vlastos claims that Aristotle confuses the notion of measurable time with the notion of temporal succession. When Aristotle argues, at *Physics* 251^b19–26, that there can be no first now, and hence that time cannot have a beginning, Vlastos complains that this shows at most that there can be no beginning to *temporal succession*. It does not show that there can be no beginning to *measurable time*. Vlastos's objection is not just that this is unfair as a criticism of Plato (since when Plato says that time has a beginning, he means *measurable time*), but also that it shows confusion on Aristotle's part. For, Vlastos claims, in defining time as a number, Aristotle himself endorses the view that time is essentially measurable. Vlastos argues that, given this definition, Aristotle should have agreed with Plato that a world without regular measurable motion would be a world without time (1965a: 386–8 and 1965b: 412–13). However, if we reject the assumption that Aristotle defines time as something measurable, there is no reason to suppose that he is confused in the way Vlastos suggests. Indeed, on the interpretation I have defended, part of Aristotle's disagreement with Plato hangs on the distinction between measurable time and temporal succession. Plato thinks time is essentially measurable, whereas Aristotle thinks it is essentially a kind of order.

PART IV

THE SAMENESS AND
DIFFERENCE OF TIMES
AND NOWS

7

All Simultaneous Time is the Same

An important question for any account of time is: what is it that makes times the same as or different from each other? Aristotle's view is that the sameness and difference of times depends on the sameness and difference of the nows that bound them. This is a consequence of his definition of time. Since time is what is counted out when we count nows, times will be the same just in case they can be counted out by counting one and the same pair of nows.

Given this view, one would expect him to provide some account of what it is for nows to be the same or different. As we have already seen, his claim that time follows change tells us something about the sameness and difference of nows. It tells us that the nows that bound earlier and later stages within any one change must be different from each other. Nows are different by being at one stage of a movement and at another (*en allō kai allō*, 219^{b}13–14).[1] However, a full account of temporal order would also have to explain the relation in which one and the same now stands to different changes. Aristotle's remarks about *following* tell us nothing about this. As we have seen, he assumes that when we count a now, we count all the change-stages that are 'at' it. This naturally raises the question: in virtue of what are these change-stages simultaneous or 'at the same now'? To this, he appears to have no answer.

Instead of explaining what it is for different change-stages to be simultaneous, he goes to some lengths to defend a certain claim about simultaneous change-stages. They are, he says, all at one and

[1] Not, as Ross has it, by being at different points in the time series. Ross (1936: 599). (Cf. Wagner (1967: 113), who translates 219^{b}13–14: 'insofern nämlich, als er selbst an verschiedenen Zeitstellen nacheinander auftritt, ist er immer ein anderer'.) In this passage Aristotle is comparing the way the now is different to the way a thing-in-motion is different. The thing-in-motion is different by being in one place then another (219^{b}21–2). The analogous point to make about the now is that it is different by being at one *movement-stage* and then another.

the same time. He puts this claim in a slightly misleading way. He says: 'all simultaneous time is the same'.[2] The expression 'simultaneous time' suggests that there can be simultaneous times that are distinct from one another, which is just what he means to deny when he says that simultaneous time is the same. We should, I think, take him to be speaking loosely here. His point is that the time of *things that are simultaneous* is one and the same.[3]

His defence of this claim depends upon a comparison between time and numbers. Just as there can be one and the same number of different equinumerous groups, so also there can be one and the same time of different changes. Both the defence and the claim defended are puzzling: the defence, because it seems to rely on the idea that time is an abstract number, rather than a number of change; the claim defended, because it is not immediately clear why it is a claim that is worth defending. Once we have agreed that certain changes are simultaneous, why is it so important to establish that they are at one and the same time?[4] I shall first explain why this claim matters to Aristotle and then go on to discuss his defence of it.

I shall argue that what is important for Aristotle is really the claim that simultaneous changes are all marked out by one and the same now. From the fact that they are marked out by the same now, it follows that these changes are all at the same time. As we have seen, the identity of a period of time depends on the identity of the nows that bound it.[5] But

[2] 219^b10 and 223^b3–4 (though see n. 5, below, for an alternative translation of 219^b10–11).

[3] As he himself points out in the *Metaphysics*, we often speak misleadingly as if one thing were two when we are discussing sameness. For instance, we treat one thing as two when we say that a thing is the same as itself (*Metaphysics* V.9.1018^{a}8–9). When he writes of 'simultaneous time' here, Aristotle is (in this sense) treating one time as two.

[4] Admittedly, my use of the English 'simultaneous' to translate the Greek '*hama*' makes this question seem particularly baffling. The Greek word is not etymologically related to the word for *same*, and it has, moreover, a broader meaning than the English 'simultaneous': two things can be *hama* (together) in place. But even when expressed in Greek, Aristotle's claim gives rise to the same question: once we have understood that the sense in which two changes are *hama* is that they are *simultaneous* (and not, for instance, that they are both occurring in the same place), what is the importance of the *extra* claim that they are both at one and the same time?

[5] As Aristotle says 'all simultaneous time is the same, for the now, whichever now it is, is the same' (219^b10–11). My translation here is controversial. Hussey (1993: 44) has: 'the whole time in sum is the same. For the now is the same X, whatever X it may be which makes it what it is' (translating '*hama*' as 'in sum'). If this is what Aristotle is

why is it so important to show that there is some *one* thing, a now, that marks all simultaneous changes?

The reason lies in Aristotle's views about the now's role in marking potential divisions in changes. As we have seen, he thinks that changes are infinitely divisible. This implies that there are infinitely many different parts into which a change could be divided. It does not, however, imply that any change in fact has all these parts. On Aristotle's view, a change does not contain infinitely many arbitrary divisions and their corresponding parts. Rather, we can create a change-part by marking a potential division in the change.[6] This view about the relation between a change and the parts into which it might be divided has important consequences for the account of time. For there is a certain natural assumption about temporal relations that depends upon the fact that changes have arbitrary parts.

It is natural to assume that if one change is occurring while another one is, the two changes will have parts that are exactly simultaneous. If I am travelling to work while the tide is rising, then there will be part of the tide's rising that is exactly simultaneous with my journey to work. In fact, this assumption is not merely natural. It is an assumption that is presupposed by Aristotle's view that time is universal: the before and after in time is an order within which all changes are related to each other. If the fact that two changes were both going on at once did not guarantee that they had parts that were exactly simultaneous, then there could be changes that stood outside the order of the before and after in time. For in that case there could be a change which had no parts that were exactly simultaneous with the parts of any other changes. In counting the parts of such a change, we would not also be counting the parts of other changes (since there would be no other change-parts that were exactly simultaneous with those that we were counting). Hence, our counting could not produce a single ordered series within which this change and all others were related.

saying, his point is not about simultaneity at all. Instead, he is saying that earlier and later times form one time series because earlier and later nows are in some way the same. However, I think this is unlikely to be the point he is making here. The expression *ho pote ēn*, which I translate 'whichever . . . it is' is not the expression that Aristotle uses elsewhere when describing the way in which earlier and later nows are the same. It is, I think, a mistake to treat *ho pote ēn* as if it were simply equivalent to the expression *ho pote on*, as Hussey does when he translates it as 'whatever X it may be which makes it what it is'. (For a discussion of these two expressions, see the Appendix.)

[6] When the division has been marked in this way, it is a *potential* division: a point at which the change might be interrupted. I have explained this view in the Introduction.

The assumption that overlapping changes have parts that are exactly simultaneous presupposes that changes have arbitrary parts. It presupposes, for instance, that if my journey to work happens while the tide is rising, then there will be a *part* of the change that is the tide's rising that is exactly simultaneous with my journey to work. Aristotle needs to show how we can make such arbitrary divisions in changes if he is to defend his assumptions about the universality of time.

The claim that one and the same now can mark potential divisions in many different changes is crucial to this defence. It implies that when we count a now, we are counting some one thing that marks all changes. In counting a now, we are *creating* boundaries within changes. What enables us to create boundaries within *all* the changes that are currently going on is just the fact that we can count some one now that they are all 'at'. Because nows are common to all changes, we do not need to mark a potential division, separately, in every change that is going on. The one act of counting the now marks potential divisions in all these changes.

This explains why it is so important to Aristotle to maintain that all simultaneous changes are at one and the same now (and hence, that they are also at one and the same time).[7] What he thinks needs to be explained here is *that there always are parts to stand in relations of simultaneity to each other* rather than, given that there are such parts, *what this relation of simultaneity between them is*. He never answers, or even raises, the question that would be central if he were giving a reductive account of temporal order. He never, that is, explains in virtue of what certain change-parts are all bounded by one and the same now.

SAMENESS AND NUMBER

Aristotle defends the claim that simultaneous changes are all at one and the same time by drawing a comparison between the sameness of times and the sameness of numbers. Just as seven dogs and seven horses are the

---

[7] The account I have sketched does, of course, raise further questions. In particular, what exactly is the role in all this of our counting? Must a now be counted in order to produce a division in the changes that are going on at it? And if so, does that mean that temporal order is, in some important way, dependent on our counting? These are questions to which I shall return in my final chapter, when I consider Aristotle's brief remarks about the relation between time and the soul.

same number, so also the time of changes that reach a limit together is the same time ($223^{b}4$–8). Many interpreters have thought this comparison indicates that there is a deep confusion at the heart of Aristotle's account.

There are two reasons why he has been thought confused on this point. First, he has already invoked the fact that equinumerous groups of different types of thing are *different* numbers in explaining how earlier and later nows can be different from one another. Such nows differ from one another, he says, just as the number of a hundred horses and that of a hundred men differ from one another ($220^{b}10$–12).[8] He seems, then, to use facts about the sameness and difference of equinumerous groups in two inconsistent ways. On the one hand, he appeals to the fact that two such groups are different numbers to explain the difference between earlier and later nows and hence between earlier and later times. On the other hand, he appeals to the fact that two equinumerous groups are, in some sense, the same number to explain how different changes can be at one and the same time.

The other reason why the comparison is often said to be confused is that it is taken to show that Aristotle is treating time as an abstract number: the number seven that is the number both of these horses and of those dogs. But the rest of his account suggests that time is not a number of *this* kind. He has defined time as a number *of change*. Moreover, when he himself discusses the sense in which numbers are the same or different, he says not that there is some one number (e.g. ten) that is the number of all groups of a certain size, but rather that all such groups are the same in kind (being all, e.g., tens) ($224^{a}12$–15). How, then, can he hope to explain the sameness of times by appealing to the idea that equinumerous groups of different kinds of thing have one and the same number? Some interpreters have concluded that in these passages he is wavering between the view that time is an abstract number and the view that it is a number of change.[9]

In fact, I shall argue, the comparison Aristotle draws here is not meant to suggest that time is an abstract number. Nor does it invoke a notion of number inconsistent with the rest of his account. Before we can understand what the comparison is meant to achieve, we need to

[8] See above pp. 94–5.
[9] This objection is made, for instance, by Hussey (1993: xli–xlii and 161).

know something more about his views on number. In what sense, for Aristotle, are two equal numbers the same?

THE SENSE IN WHICH TWO EQUAL NUMBERS ARE THE SAME OR DIFFERENT

Right at the end of his account, Aristotle explains in what sense two equal numbers are or are not the same as each other.[10] It is worth looking in detail at what he says:

(i) It is rightly said that the number of the sheep and of the dogs is the same, if each number is equal, but the ten is not the same nor are they the same ten,

(ii) just as the equilateral and scalene are not the same triangles, though they are the same figure, since both are triangles.

(iii) Things are said to be the same X if they do not differ by the difference of an X, but not [the same X] if they do,

(iv) for example, a triangle differs from a triangle by the difference of a triangle, and therefore they are different triangles; but they do not [differ by the difference] of a figure, but are in one and the same division [of figure]. For one kind of figure is a circle, another a triangle, and one kind of triangle is equilateral, another is scalene. So they are the same figure, that is, a triangle, but not the same triangle;

(v) and so, it is the same number, since the number of them does not differ by the difference of a number, but not the same ten, since the things it is said of are different: dogs in the one case, horses in the other. (224^a2-15)[11]

Aristotle is not at his most readable here, but it is possible, with patience, to tease out what he means. He starts from the obvious point that there is some sense in which the number of ten sheep and the number of ten dogs is the 'same'. His question is: what is the sense of 'same' here?

To answer this, he lays down a general principle (iii). A and B are the same X if and only if they are both Xs and do not differ in respect of the differentia that falls immediately under the class of Xs (or, as he puts

---

[10] That he is prepared to write of 'equal numbers' (224^a3) is itself revealing. Two groups of ten are two numbers, tens, that are equal to each other.

[11] Aristotle, confusingly, switches his example from ten sheep and ten dogs, at the beginning of the passage, to ten horses and ten dogs, at the end.

it, they 'do not differ by the difference of an X'). The example he uses to illustrate this principle, at (iv), helps us to understand what he means by it. Scalene and equilateral triangles are, he says, the same figure but not the same triangle. They differ in so far as they are triangles, since one of them is scalene and the other equilateral, but they are not different types of figure, since they are both triangles. A diagram is useful here.

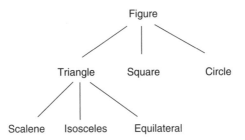

As the diagram shows, the first divisions of the genus figure are into the species triangle, square, circle, and so on. Scalene and equilateral triangles are the same figure because they both belong in the same one of these species (in the species triangle). In other words, scalene and equilateral triangles are figures that 'do not differ by the difference of a figure'. The reason why they are not the same triangle is that the first division of the genus *triangle* is into scalene, isosceles, and equilateral. There is thus no species of the genus triangle into which both scalene and equilateral triangles fall. In other words, 'they differ by the difference of a triangle'.

We can now use this principle to explain the sense in which ten dogs is the same as ten sheep. Aristotle wants to say that ten dogs and ten sheep are different types of ten but not different types of number. Again, a diagram may help:

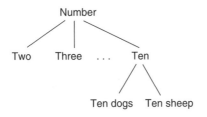

Aristotle tells us (at v) that ten dogs and ten sheep do not differ by the difference of a number. His view must be that number is like a genus.[12] The first division of this genus is into the species two, three . . . nine, ten, and so on. Ten dogs and ten sheep are both numbers and they both fall within the same species of this first division of number (since they are both tens), so they do not 'differ by the difference of a number'. They are, then, the same number (or, in other words, the same kind of number). Ten dogs and ten sheep are not, however, the same kind of ten. This is because they differ by the difference of a ten. Aristotle is here treating the number ten as a genus. The first divisions of this genus are into groups of different kinds of units: ten sheep, ten horses, ten men, etc. Ten dogs and ten sheep are thus both tens, but they fall into different first species of the genus ten. It follows that ten dogs and ten sheep are numbers of the same kind but not tens of the same kind. As Aristotle puts it (at v) they are 'the same number' but 'not the same ten'.[13]

This passage, then, suggests that ten sheep and ten dogs are the same number in that they fall into the same class *number* (just as scalene and equilateral are the same figure, in that they both fall into the same class *figure*). To say that they are the same number is not to imply that there is some one thing, the abstract number ten, that is the number of each.[14]

THERE IS ONE TIME OF SIMULTANEOUS CHANGES, JUST AS THERE IS ONE NUMBER OF SEVEN DOGS AND SEVEN HORSES

I have argued that, for Aristotle, the sense in which two equinumerous groups 'have the same number' is not that there is some one abstract number that is the number of each. Given this view of number, how can he

[12] There are at least two reasons for denying that it actually is a genus. First, such a genus would be divided into infinitely many species. Second, it would be a genus of things that stand in a before-and-after order and Aristotle thinks that there can be no genus of such things. (See for example *Metaphysics* III.3.999ª6 ff, *De Anima* II.3.414ᵇ20 ff, *Nicomachean Ethics* I.6.1096ª17 ff, and *Politics* III.1.1275ª35 ff)

[13] Ten dogs and ten other dogs would be the same ten (in the sense that they would be the same kind of ten).

[14] It is sometimes claimed that the Greeks never think of number in this abstract way (as, for instance, the number six, rather than a group of six units). See Burnyeat (1990: 205–9), Pritchard (1995: p. 1), Klein (1968). My interpretation here is consistent with this claim, but does not presuppose it.

use the fact that seven dogs and seven horses are the same number to explain the sameness of changes that reach a limit together? After all, he thinks that changes that reach a limit together *are* all at one and the same period of time. The answer, I think, is that he invokes the fact that equinumerous groups have the same number only to answer a potential objection to his view that there is one time for simultaneous changes. In doing this, he does not imply that there is some abstract number seven that is the number of all groups of seven, in the way that there is some one time period that is the time of every member of a set of simultaneous changes.

In the passage in which he makes this point, he emphasizes that time is a number of every kind of change: of coming to be, ceasing to be, growth, qualitative change, and locomotion. 'Time is a number of continuous change *simpliciter*, not of one particular type' (223^a33–223^b1). From this view that time is a number of every kind of change, someone might draw the conclusion that there must be different kinds of time corresponding to each different kind of change. This would suggest an objection to his claim that simultaneous changes are at one and the same time. If for each different kind of change there was a different kind of time, then whenever two changes of different kinds were simultaneous, there would be two different kinds of time (and hence two different times) together. As he puts the objection:

But it is possible that now another thing has also changed. So that of each of these changes there would be a number. So will there be a different time and two equal times together?   (223^b1–3)

This objection depends on the assumption that there must be a different kind of number for each type of thing numbered.[15] It is this assumption that Aristotle is criticizing when he says that seven dogs and seven horses are, in a sense, the same number. His point is that numbers can be the same

---

[15] It might seem that this assumption is not worth taking so seriously. But if one reflects upon the great variety of things that can be counted (not just horses and dogs, but also things in other categories, like moves in chess, holes in a piece of cheese, and colours of nail polish) it can come to seem remarkable that things of such different kinds are comparable in respect of plurality. After all, we could not compare such things in respect of *goodness*. (It does not make sense to ask: 'is the goodness of this *good opening move in chess* as great as the goodness of that *good colour of nail polish?*') There is, then, some reason for Aristotle to make a point of explaining that *three opening moves in chess* and *three colours of nail polish* can both be the same kind of number, even though they are different kinds of three. (Interestingly, there is a passage in the *Physics* VII, where he himself suggests that 'one' is homonymous, and that if 'one' is, so is 'two', 248^b19–21.)

in kind though they are numbers of different kinds of thing. This follows from the claims that we have already encountered about the sameness and difference of numbers. Two sevens fall into the same genus, though they are numbers of different kinds of thing—of horses and of dogs:

> For time that is equal and simultaneous is one and the same. And even those which are not simultaneous are the same in kind. For if there were dogs and horses, seven of each, there would be the same number. Thus, also of changes that reach a limit together there is the same time, even if one is quick another not, and one is movement and another alteration.   (223^{b}3–8)

From the fact that changes are of different kinds, it does not follow that their times are of different kinds. Even non-simultaneous changes that are of different kinds are not, because of this, at different kinds of time (223^{b}4).

If different kinds of change can be at the same kind of time, then we are not forced to say that there are two different simultaneous times whenever two different kinds of change are going on simultaneously. Hence, the fact that there are different kinds of change does not threaten Aristotle's view that all time that is equal and together is the same.[16]

I have argued that Aristotle only makes this point about sameness of number in order to undermine one reason for thinking that there could be two distinct but simultaneous times. But does he have any more positive explanation of how it is possible for there to be one time of many different changes? He may be hinting at such an explanation in a somewhat strange remark he makes at the end of the passage we have been considering (223^{b}10–12). In this remark, he compares the time of simultaneous changes not just to equal numbers, but to the numbers of things that are equal and *together* (*hama*).

NUMBERS OF THINGS THAT ARE EQUAL AND TOGETHER

Time is everywhere the same, he says, because also the number is one and the same of things that are equal and together:

---

[16] Note that, in this passage, Aristotle again speaks of time that is 'together' (*hama*). Again, we have to take him to be speaking loosely (as I explained above, p. 114).

... though changes are different and separate from each other, time is everywhere the same, because the number too of things equal and together is one and the same everywhere.   (223^{b}10–12)

I have explained the sense in which equinumerous groups of different kinds of thing have the same number. But what can Aristotle mean by this claim that the number of things that are equal and *together* (or simultaneous: *hama*) is one and the same?[17] Surely, the number of things that are equal is the same (in whatever sense it is the same), regardless of whether those things are together.

It is possible that the word 'together' here is just a slip. In that case, he is simply repeating his point that two equinumerous groups have the same kind of number. But there is also a more interesting possibility. Aristotle could be making a new claim. He could be claiming that the fact that certain groups are not just equal but also *together* implies that there is some other, stronger sense in which they have one and the same number. What might he mean by this?

Any answer to this must necessarily be speculative. But there is one possibility that accords very well with the interpretation that I have been presenting. It depends on the idea that collections of things can be arranged in such a way that we are able to count several different collections in one and the same act of counting. For instance, if a collection of seven horses is paired with a collection of seven men, one man on each horse, then we can count the horses and the men together. Suppose we are using a collection of seven pebbles to count with. We can use these pebbles to count at the same time both the horses and the men. This is the sense in which there can be one number of things that are equal and together. In the case of changes, it is when they are together (in the sense of being simultaneous) that we can count several of them with just one action of counting. Just as we could use the same seven pebbles to count both the horses and the men on them, so also we can use the same now to count any changes that are simultaneous.

If this is right, then Aristotle is saying that there is one time of changes that are equal and together just because they can (like a group of men paired with a group of horses) be counted in one and the same act of counting. The group of nows serves as a kind of number with

[17] As I have already explained, the word *hama* can mean simultaneous (i.e. together in time) and can also mean together in other ways (e.g. together in place).

which we count. We can count changes that are equal and together using one and the same group of nows. Because of this, all such changes are at one and the same time.

Further evidence that Aristotle thinks of nows in this way is provided by a difficult passage at the end of chapter 11. In this passage, he describes the now as a kind of number with which we count. He connects this, in a way that he does not make explicit, with the fact that there can be one and the same number of different equinumerous groups of things:

So in so far as the now is a limit, it is not time, but an attribute of time, but in so far as it counts, it is a number. (For the limits are only of that of which they are limits, but the number of these horses, the ten, is elsewhere too.)   (220^{a}21–4)

His point, I think, is that though the now is not time, it has a special role in time. A series of nows is a kind of number with which we count change. The now, if it is to count change, must be more than a mere limit. If nows were simply limits of changes, then each now would be defined in terms of some particular change that it limited. It is because the nows are a number with which we count change that it is possible to count all simultaneous changes with one and the same now. When we count a now, we are counting divisions in all the changes that are going on at it. So when we count out ten nows, we are counting many different tens. Just as we could use the same group of ten things, e.g. ten pebbles, to count ten horses and ten dogs, so we can use these ten nows to count ten divisions in this change and ten divisions in that other change.[18]

---

[18] My interpretation does not solve all the difficulties about this passage. It is odd to find Aristotle saying that the now (as opposed to a series of counted *nows*) is a number. Moreover, it is not clear quite what he means when he says that the ten of these horses is 'also elsewhere'. On my interpretation, what one would expect him to say is that the ten that is the number we use to count these horses could also be used to count ten things of some other kind (for instance, ten dogs).

8

The Sameness of Earlier and Later Times and Nows

The account I have attributed to Aristotle relies heavily on claims about the now. It is by counting nows that we count time. Because one and the same now is the now of many different changes, in counting a now, we divide all the changes that are occurring at it. Moreover, the identity of times depends on the nows that bound them: earlier and later times are different because they are counted out by different nows; the time of things that are simultaneous is the same because it is bounded by one and the same pair of nows. We have seen, then, that the now has an important role in Aristotle's account of time. It remains for us to consider what the now must be like if it is to play this role.

'The now', Aristotle says, 'is in a way the same always and in a way not the same' ($219^b12–13$). In the last chapter, we saw that one and the same now could divide different simultaneous changes; here, I am concerned with the sameness and difference of earlier and later nows. It turns out that there are two distinct ways in which earlier and later nows are the same. They are the same in definition, in that they are all nows, but they are also the same in another, less obvious way. That they should be the same in this second way is, I shall argue, of central importance in Aristotle's account. It is only because they are the same in this way that it is possible to count them.

This discussion of the now is one of the most difficult parts of his account. It is difficult partly because, in it, he makes heavy use of two analogies, each of which is potentially misleading. He compares the now's relation to time on the one hand to the relation of a point to a line and, on the other hand, to the relation of a thing-in-motion to its motion. Because this discussion is so difficult to follow, I shall first lay out what I take to be Aristotle's views about the sameness and difference of earlier and later nows and only then go on to look at the two analogies by means of which he explains them.[1]

TWO WAYS IN WHICH EARLIER AND LATER NOWS ARE THE SAME

(1) The Same (and yet Different) in *Logos*

One sense in which all nows are the same is, simply, that they are all nows. They are all, that is, the same in *logos* or definition.[2] To be a now is to be something that lies between the past and the future. As Aristotle says, 'the now is a link (*sunecheia*) of time, for it binds together the past and the future' (222ª10–11).

Earlier and later nows are also different from each other. They are different in being (*einai*) (219ᵇ27). It is interesting to note that the difference between earlier and later nows is intimately bound up with their sameness. Each now, when it is, unites a past to a future. In that respect, the nows are all the same. But for each now, there is a different past and a different future. Because of this, though each now unites a past to a future, what it is for the now to unite the past to the future is, in each case, different. As I shall explain, this relation between the sameness and the difference of earlier and later nows has a parallel in the relation between the sameness and difference of earlier and later stages of a thing-in-motion.[3]

(2) That, by Being which the Now is, is the Same

There is also a second way in which earlier and later nows are the same as each other. Aristotle expresses this second way in which the nows are

---

[1] The plausibility of my interpretation of Aristotle's views on the sameness and difference of nows depends partly on its ability to make sense of these analogies. Hence, some of the evidence for claims I make in the next section comes in my discussion of the analogies, later in the chapter.

[2] Aristotle points out that the thing-in-motion also, in a sense, remains the same in definition (220ª7–8).

[3] The reason why I use this contrived term 'thing-in-motion', rather than the more natural 'moving thing' will become clear below (pp. 134–8). As I shall explain, 'thing-in-motion' refers to an entity that is by definition in motion, as opposed to something that happens to be moving.

the same using an odd phrase. He says that '*that, whatever it is, by being which the now is,* is the same' (219ᵇ14–15).[4] Before we can understand the point he is making here, we need to see why he thinks it important to show that the nows are the same, not just in definition, but also in some further way.

This is important because if time is to be a number, earlier and later nows must be countable. Aristotle twice compares the now to a unit.[5] When we count the members of a collection, the units we count must all be in some respect the same. That is just what it is for them to be units in a countable collection. In order for us to count, we must be able to give some answer to the question 'what is it that you are counting?'. As we have seen, there is something odd about counting *nows*: the nows we count do not exist independently of our counting. There is a sense in which we create the series of nows by counting it. Nevertheless, there must be some description of what it is that we are creating and counting. If the nows we are creating are countable, there must, independently of our counting, be some respect in which they are all the same.

The fact that the nows we count are the same in *definition* cannot be what provides this basis for counting them. As we have seen, for the nows to be the same in definition is for each of them to unite a past with a future. But the possibility of uniting a past with a future itself depends on there being a countable series of nows. This is because there can only be a past and a future to be united by the now, if there is a countable before and after in time.[6] If there were no such before and after in time, there might still be a distinction between *being past* and *being future,*[7] but there could not be a single ordered series of times stretching further and further into the past and another ordered series of times stretching

---

[4] For a discussion of this phrase, see the Appendix.

[5] *Physics* IV.11.220ᵃ4 and 12.221ᵃ13–15.

[6] This is one of the reasons why time's relation to a now is not like a line's relation to a point on that line. Two segments of a line can be joined at a point, just as the past and the future are joined at a now. But each segment of the line exists as a unity whether or not any points are marked out in it, whereas there can be neither a unified past nor a unified future unless there is a before and after series of nows.

[7] As I shall explain in Ch. 10, there can only be a *countable* before and after in time, if a before and after in time is in fact *counted*. But on Aristotle's view, whether or not a particular event is past or future must, surely, be independent of our counting. After all, he says elsewhere that everything that is either past or present is necessary, whereas some future events are not yet necessary (*De Interpretatione* 9).

further and further into the future.[8] In that sense, there could not be either *a* past or *a* future. It follows that the nows are only the same in definition—they are only things that unite a past with a future—because they are countable. As Aristotle says, it is because the before and after is countable that the now is what it is.[9] The fact that nows are the same in definition cannot, then, be a precondition for their countability. This, I think, is the reason why Aristotle is at some pains to show that earlier and later nows are not merely the same in the sense that they are all nows but are also the same in some other way. He tells us that *that, whatever it is, by being which the now is* is the same.

What does he mean by this? A clue comes in one of the passages in which he compares the now to a thing-in-motion. He says there:

> *That, whatever it is, by being which the now is* is the same (for it is the before and after in change). But its being is different: it is in so far as the before and after is countable that the now is [what it is].   (219^b26–8)

When he writes of *that, whatever it is, by being which the now is* Aristotle means to refer to what it is about the now that holds independently of its countability. If we abstract from the fact that nows are countable (and hence also from their relation to time), what we are left with is the nows' relation to change. The nows form a series of before and after potential divisions in changes. It is by being before and after in change that the now is what it is. When we count nows, what we are doing is counting before and after potential divisions in changes in a certain way. The earlier and later nows we count are all the same in that they are all

---

[8] An interesting consequence of my interpretation here is that Aristotle is committed to the view that if there were no before and after in time, there might be a distinction between being past and being future, but there could not be what modern philosophers (following McTaggart) have called an 'A series'. There would not be an ordered series stretching further and further into the future and an ordered series stretching further and further into the past.

[9] 219^b25, 219^b28. He says 'in so far as the before and after is countable, the now is'. I take this to mean, not just that the now exists because the before and after is countable, but also that the now's being what it is (a now) depends on the countability of the before and after. There is an alternative possible translation of this line. It could be translated: 'the now is the before and after, considered as countable' (see, e.g. Hussey (1993: 45)). However, my interpretation does not depend upon the translation of this line. The position I attribute to Aristotle here also follows from other things he says. It follows from his view that the now is essentially a unifier of the past with the future (222^a10–11), together with the view that there cannot be a past or a future to be unified unless there is a single countable before and after in time.

potential divisions we make in changes. That is, every now that we count is a potential division in the before and after in some change or other. Of course, there is a sense in which even this way of being the same depends on our counting. We create potential divisions in changes as we count them. But the important point, for Aristotle's purposes, is that *what it is to be a potential division in a change* can be explained independently of any reference to our counting: a potential division is a point at which a change might be interrupted. To count nows is to create and count such potential divisions.

In what sense, though, is *being a potential division in some change or other* a way of being the same? Aristotle distinguishes between several different ways of being the same in his philosophical dictionary in *Metaphysics* V. One way of being the same is to be 'one by analogy'.[10] Things are one by analogy which are related 'as one thing is to another (*allo pros allo*)' (1016^{b}34–5). An example Aristotle gives elsewhere is that the straight line and the plane are one by analogy because 'as the straight line is in length, so is the plane in surface' (*Metaphysics* XIV.6.1093^{b}18–20). This, I think, is the way in which earlier and later nows are the same. As one now N1 is to the before and after in change C1, so another now N2 is to the before and after in change C2. N1 and N2 are the same in that each is the marker of the before and after in some change. When we count nows we are counting markers of potential divisions in changes.

THE TWO ANALOGIES BY WHICH ARISTOTLE ILLUSTRATES HIS ACCOUNT OF THE NOW

Aristotle uses two analogies to explain the ways in which earlier and later nows are the same. He uses an analogy between the now and a point on a line to illustrate the fact that any now binds together a past and a future. Just as all points on the line unite two sections of the line, so all nows unite a past with a future. However, the now's relation to time is

---

[10] He says, in *Metaphysics* V.9, that 'things are said to be *per se* the same in as many ways as they are said to be one' (V.9.1018^{a}4–5); that is, for each way of being one, there is a corresponding way of being the same. He discusses the different senses in which things can be one in *Metaphysics* V.6. Among them, he lists *being one by analogy* (1016^{b}31–2).

not quite like a point's relation to a line. Different nows are the same as each other in a further way in which points on a line are not. In order to illustrate the other respect in which nows are all the same, he relies upon a different analogy. For this, he turns to an analogy between the now and a moving point, or, more generally, between the now and a thing-in-motion. A thing-in-motion is, like the now, the same in two different respects. As it passes through different change-stages, the thing-in-motion is not only the same in definition, but also the same in respect of that being which it is.

THE NOW'S RELATION TO TIME AND A POINT'S RELATION TO A LINE

We looked earlier at Aristotle's view that there are structural correspondences between time, a movement, and a line.[11] His account of the now implies that it is an indivisible boundary that unites the past and the future and divides the past from the future. Given this description, it is very natural to picture time as a line and the now as a point on the line. Already, in the puzzles at the beginning of his account, he has raised some difficulties with this picture. In his discussion of the now, he claims that there are important differences between a line's relation to a point on it and time's relation to the now.[12]

A point on a line can both divide the line into two parts and join the line together. The point can do this because it is a limit of each part of the line: 'it is the beginning of one and the end of the other' (220^a11). Similarly the now makes time continuous (it binds together the past and the future) and it is a limit of time, being (at least, in a sense) the end of the past and the beginning of the future (222^a10-12). This much the now and the point have in common. But there are nevertheless important respects in which they are different. A line can actually be divided at a point on it. For instance, we can cut the line in half and separate the two halves. Or, in a movement over the line, we can stop at the point and then move on again (220^a12-13).[13] But time cannot in the same

[11] See Part II.
[12] IV.11, 220^a10-21, IV.12, 222^a10-20.
[13] By doing this, Aristotle thinks, we create a kind of double boundary. Any double boundary of this sort makes an actual division in the line.

sense be divided at the now. The now is always different, so we cannot stop at the now, making of it an end and a beginning (220ᵃ13–15).

This raises a question. In what sense does the now divide the past from the future? Aristotle says that it 'divides potentially' (222ᵃ13–14). It divides potentially because it can mark a boundary in change, and hence in time, even though it cannot make this boundary into a beginning and an end. As I said in the Introduction, Aristotle must be relying here on the analogy between the now and a point. A point that has been marked on a line but at which nothing has stopped is a potential division on the line. It marks the line into two parts but does not actually divide the parts from one another. Similarly, a now is a potential division in time since it marks the time into two parts, though it does not (and in fact cannot) actually divide the parts from one another.[14]

The now also has a role in unifying time that the point does not have in unifying the line. As we have seen, there is a sense in which the point unifies the line. If there is to be one line instead of two, the point that is the end of one half of it must also be the beginning of the other half. But on Aristotle's view, the line is prior to the point: the line can exist as a unity whether or not we create a point on it by marking out a potential division. Moreover, when two line segments are joined at a point, each segment itself exists as a unity whether or not we mark points on it. Time is not, in this way, prior to the now. The unity of time depends, in part, on our counting nows.[15] Because of this, different nows need to be the same in a sense in which different stationary points on a line do not. They must be the same in some way that does not depend on their relation to time.

To illustrate this further way in which nows are the same, Aristotle invokes a different view of the relation between a point and a line. Certain mathematicians, he says, think that a line is what is traced out by a moving point (13.222ᵃ14–17). Aristotle himself does not share this view. But he uses it nevertheless as a model for the relation between time and the now.

---

[14] For all this, see my discussion of divisions in time and in change in the Introduction. As I said there, it is somewhat puzzling that Aristotle thinks it makes sense to say that something divides potentially when that thing could never divide actually.

[15] As I explained above, pp. 127–8, there cannot even be a unified past or a unified future, unless there is a before and after series of nows.

The now is the same in something like the way in which (on this mathematicians' view) a point tracing out a line is always the same point. It is because the now remains the same in this way that it is able to tie together time and make it a unity:

It [the now] divides potentially. And in so far as it is such, the now is always different. But in so far as it ties together it is always the same, just as in the case of mathematical lines (for it is not always the same point in thought. For it divides in one place and another. But in so far as it is one, it is the same everywhere). (222ᵃ14–17)

This analogy between the now and a moving point is, in fact, just a specific instance of a more general analogy that Aristotle develops at greater length. For a full understanding of Aristotle's views on the sameness of earlier and later nows we need to turn to his discussion of the analogy between a now and a thing-in-motion.

THE NOW AND THE THING-IN-MOTION

He draws an extended analogy between the now and a thing-in-motion. The now remains the same while being 'different and different' just as a thing-in-motion remains the same, while it is different by being in one place and another (219ᵇ13–22). In fact, the now is like a thing-in-motion in a number of ways. We know time by the now, just as we know movement by means of a thing-in-motion (219ᵇ28–31). The now unites and divides time just as a thing-in-motion unites and divides a movement (220ᵃ4–9). And the now and time are together (*hama*), as are the thing-in-motion and its movement (220ᵃ1–3).[16]

Not surprisingly, the fact that he draws this analogy has often been taken to show that he thinks the now is itself something that moves, constantly progressing in a futurely direction.[17] On this view, there is just one now. This now is always different in the sense that at each moment it is a different dated instant. If this were what Aristotle meant

---

[16] I take Aristotle's odd expression 'the number of the thing-in-motion' (220ᵃ2–3) to refer to the now. The thought, perhaps, is that when we count the now, we count whatever stage of the thing-in-motion is at the now. In that sense, the now is the number of the thing-in-motion.

[17] This is Hussey's view (1993: see especially xliii–xlvi and 152–7).

to say, then the account I have given above of the sameness and difference of nows would be mistaken. As we shall see, there are many reasons for doubting the moving-now interpretation. But if we reject this interpretation, we are left with the difficult task of explaining how Aristotle does mean us to understand the analogy between the now and a moving thing.

An important reason for doubting the moving-now interpretation is that it ascribes to Aristotle a view that is incompatible with two of his other doctrines. First, he says elsewhere that things that are indivisible cannot move. Since he thinks that the now is indivisible, this implies that the now too cannot move.[18] Second, as we have already seen, he claims that time is not a kind of movement.[19] His argument for this was that if time were a movement, then it would have to be the sort of thing that could be faster or slower. A parallel argument could be given against the view that the now moves: if the now were something that moved, its movement would have to be the sort of thing that could be faster or slower.

These considerations don't themselves provide a decisive reason for rejecting a moving-now interpretation. After all, a general claim, made at the beginning of the argument, may turn out to need modification as the argument progresses. But there is no indication in the text that Aristotle thinks *these* two claims should be modified. He does not, for instance, explain that there is a particular kind of movement (the movement of the now) that need not be faster or slower. Nor does he argue that the now is special in some way that allows it to move even though it is indivisible.

There is, in any case, an independent reason for rejecting the moving-now interpretation. The language with which Aristotle expresses his claim about the sameness of the now suggests that he does not mean to imply that the now is something that moves. He says that *that, whatever it is, by being which the now is* (*ho de pote on esti to nun*) is the same (219^{b}14–15). This phrase '*ho pote on X estin*' is hard to construe and just what Aristotle means by it is controversial.[20] But whatever he means by it, it clearly is not his standard way to refer to the way in which

---

[18] *Physics* VI.10 240^{b}8–241^{a}26.
[19] *Physics* IV.10 218^{b}9–18. See above Ch. 2.
[20] I explain my interpretation of it in the Appendix.

untitled

something remains the same through change.[21] His usual way to describe the way in which the subject of a change remains the same is to say that the underlying thing, or *hupokeimenon*, remains one and the same in number but is not one and the same in form.[22] The fact that he does not say this in his discussion of the sameness of nows is in itself a prima facie reason to doubt that he is straightforwardly claiming that the now is a kind of moving thing.[23]

But if, as I have been arguing, Aristotle is not simply claiming that the now is a kind of moving thing, what is the point of the analogy? How does the comparison of the now with a thing-in-motion help us to understand the sameness and difference of earlier and later nows? How, indeed, is it possible for the now to be the same and different in the way that a thing-in-motion is the same and different, without itself being something that moves?

In order to answer these questions, we need to look more carefully at Aristotle's claims about the thing-in-motion. I want to argue that in this context Aristotle is not using the term '*pheromenon*', which I have been translating 'thing-in-motion', as he normally would, to refer to the subject of a movement: the thing that happens to be moving.[24] He is not, that is, referring to some concrete particular—a stone, Coriscos, etc.—which is first in one place and then moves to another place. On his standard view, when a stone moves from A to B, the stone remains what it is (a stone) throughout the movement and it is first at A and then at B. Similarly, with other kinds of non-substantial change. If Coriscos changes from being pale to being dark, then one and the same thing,

---

[21] In our passage Aristotle does say that that being which the *pheromenon* (thing-in-motion) is remains the same through the change, but I shall argue that '*pheromenon*' here must be understood in a special sense.

[22] See, for example, *Physics* I.7.190ᵃ15–16.

[23] A further disadvantage of the moving-now interpretation is that it has very little to say about the relation between Aristotle's claim that the now remains the same and the rest of his account. On the interpretation I have proposed, the claim that earlier and later nows are in some way the same is essential to the overall view that time is a countable number. Hussey (who puts forward a moving-now interpretation) says that the claim that the now remains the same has no function within the rest of Aristotle's account. It is, he suggests, a claim Aristotle accepts solely because of the phenomenology of time: 'in accepting the existence of a persistent present Aristotle complicates his theory considerably. The fact must be that Aristotle thinks he has to accept the notion of a permanent present as given in the phenomenology of the subject. The notion does no further work within Aristotle's system' (Hussey 1993: xliv).

[24] That is why I have been using the odd translation 'thing-in-motion'.

Coriscos, first has the property of paleness and then, at the end of the change, the property of darkness.

That this is not what he means by thing-in-motion can be inferred from the first passage in which he talks of the sameness and difference of the thing-in-motion. He says there:

> This [the thing-in-motion] is the same in respect of that, whatever it is, by being which it is (for it is a point or stone or something else of this sort), but it is different in account, just as the sophists assume that being Coriscos in the Lyceum is different from being Coriscos in the market.   ($219^{b}18$–21)

Point and stone here are examples of 'that, whatever it is, by being which [the thing-in-motion] is'. What he seems to be saying is that when a stone or a point moves from A to B, *that by being which the thing-in-motion is* (i.e. the stone or the point) remains the same.[25] *That by being which the thing-in-motion is* is, then, the subject of the movement (i.e. the thing that moves). Aristotle uses the phrase 'that being which X is' in such a way as to distinguish between X and that being which X is.[26] So there is good reason to think that what Aristotle calls the 'thing-in-motion' (*pheromenon*) is distinct from *that by being which the thing-in-motion is*. In other words, the 'thing-in-motion' is distinct from the subject of the movement.

If this is right, then by 'the thing-in-motion' Aristotle must be referring to something that is distinct from (though closely related to) the thing (such as the stone or the point) that happens to be in movement. My proposal is that 'the thing-in-motion', as he uses the term here, is something that is *defined* as being in movement: not *this stone* but *this-stone-in-movement-from-A-to-B*.[27] When he says that the thing-in-motion remains the same in a way because *that by being which it is*, namely the \subject of the movement, remains the same, his point is that the sameness of *this-stone-in-movement-from-A-to-B* depends on the sameness of *this stone*.

Some support for this proposal can be found in Aristotle's remarks about the way in which Coriscos remains the same. He says that the thing-in-motion is different in the way that *the sophists* say that Coriscos'

---

[25] Aristotle is appealing here to the view that a point is something that creates a line by moving, a view that, as we have seen, he invokes more explicitly at $222^{a}15$–17.

[26] See Appendix.

[27] The proposal is also defended by Broadie (1984).

being in the market and Coriscos' being in the Lyceum are different. If he were thinking of a thing-in-motion as a subject of movement, he could simply have said that it was different as Coriscos is different by being in one place and then another. Why, then, this mention of the sophists? Aristotle says elsewhere that the sophists are concerned above all with the accidental and he cites, as an example of a sophistic puzzle, the question whether Coriscos and musical Coriscos are the same.[28] The sophistic argument that he is referring to in our passage of the *Physics* is probably something like the following. '*Being in the market* is different from *being in the Lyceum*. Coriscos is first in the market and then in the Lyceum, so Coriscos becomes different from himself'. Aristotle's stand-ard response to an argument of this sort would be to say that it mistakes an accidental for an essential difference. Coriscos is essentially a man and he remains the same man while undergoing change in place.[29] In this passage, though, Aristotle is not using the term '*pheromenon*' (or 'thing-in-motion'), as he standardly does, to refer to something like Coriscos that moves. Instead, the thing-in-motion to which he is referring is *Coriscos-in-movement-from-the-market-to-the-Lyceum*. It is not merely an accidental feature of the entity *Coriscos-in-movement-from-the-market-to-the-Lyceum* that it is always different. Rather, this (somewhat strange) entity can only remain the kind of thing it is by being always in different places. This explains why he invokes the sophistic view about the way in which a thing-in-motion is always different. The now is analogous to a thing-in-motion *as such a thing would be conceived by the sophists*.[30]

Understanding 'thing-in-motion' in this way also helps to make sense of an otherwise puzzling remark he makes later. The thing-in-motion

---

[28] *Metaphysics* VI.2.1026^{b}15–21.

[29] He emphasizes in the *Categories* that a substance is something that can remain one and the same in number, while having at different times different accidental properties. For example, an individual man, remaining one and the same, can be pale at one time and dark at another (*Categories* 5. 4^{a}17–21).

[30] It is interesting that both of the analogies Aristotle draws to illustrate his views about the now make use of theories that he himself does not accept. As we have seen, he compares the relation between time and the now to the relation between a line and the point that traces out the line (according to certain mathematicians) (222^{a}15–17). And he also compares the relation between time and the now to the relation between a move-ment and a moving thing (as the moving thing is thought of by the sophists) (219^{b}19–21). His reliance on such analogies reflects, I think, the difficulty he has in spelling out this further way in which earlier and later nows are all the same.

and motion are together, he says, in the way that the now and time are together (220^a1–2).This remark suggests that a thing-in-motion cannot exist without its movement (just as the now cannot exist without time) (219^b33–220^a1). If by 'thing-in-motion' Aristotle meant the thing, e.g. Coriscos, that happened to be moving, this remark would be very hard to explain. Coriscos still exists when his movement to the market is over. But the comparison he is drawing makes clear sense if we take 'thing-in-motion' to mean: thing defined as in movement. *Coriscos-moving-from-the-Lyceum-to-the-market* is an entity that only exists together with the movement.

Aristotle says that the thing-in-motion is what makes the movement one. To do this, it must remain the same in account (*logos*): the movement is one because the thing-in-motion is one, 'and not because *that, whatever it is, by being which it is* (*ho pote on*) is one, for that might leave a gap, but one in account (*logos*)' (220^a6–8). The reason why it is not enough for the moving thing to remain the same in respect of *that, by being which, it is* is that the movement might stop, even though the subject of the movement remained the same. For example, Coriscos could still persist even if there was a gap in his movement to the market. On the other hand, *Coriscos-moving-from-the-Lyceum-to-the-market* is not something that could persist through such a gap. So there will be one unified movement just in case the thing-in-motion (e.g. *Coriscos-moving-from-the-Lyceum-to-the-market*) remains the same in *logos*.[31]

Of course, for the thing-in-motion to remain what it is (that is, to remain the same in account), it must also, in another sense, be always different in account. Coriscos-moving-from-the-Lyceum-to-the-market can only remain what it is by being first Coriscos-in-motion-through-point-P1, then Coriscos-in-motion-through-point-P2, and so on. The thing-in-motion is different 'by being in one place and another' (219^b21–2). It is a strange kind of entity that, like Heraclitus' posset, can only remain the same by being ever different.[32]

---

[31] This account of this passage is developed by Broadie (1984: 121). For an alternative, see Hussey (1993: 158).

[32] This strange entity, the thing-in-motion, is introduced partly as a response to a problem for Aristotle's project here. The problem is that he needs some account of what it is for one and the same change to continue without gaps. Elsewhere, he says that if a change is to be one it must (among other things) take place in one continuous time (*Physics* V.4.227^b29–228^a1). If, for instance, the change starts at 2 p.m. and ends at 3 p.m., then it must be going on during all the intermediate periods of time. This is what

This thing-in-motion, Aristotle tells us, is that by which we know the before and after in change (219^{b}23–5). The fact that it is the same and yet different in the way I have described explains how it can have this role. We know that the earlier and later stages of a movement differ from each other by recognizing the way in which the thing-in-motion is different in *logos*; we know that they are all stages of one and the same movement by recognizing the way in which the thing-in-motion remains the same in *logos*.

I have argued that when Aristotle compares the now to a 'thing-in-motion', he is drawing an analogy between the now and this strange entity: *the thing defined as in motion* (or, as I have called it, the 'thing-in-motion'). With this in mind, it is possible to see the parallels between the sameness and difference of the thing-in-motion and the sameness and difference of earlier and later nows.

The thing-in-motion is, like earlier and later nows, the same in two different respects. One way in which the nows are the same is that they are the same in definition or account (*logos*). As we have seen, the now is something that only remains the same in *logos* by being always different in *logos*. It is the same, in that it is always what unites the past and the future. It is different in that it is always uniting a different past to a different future. The thing-in-motion too is something that is always different in *logos* (219^{b}19–22) but is also, in a way, always the same in *logos* (220^{a}7–8). Like the now, it is an entity that only remains the same in *logos* (only remains, say, Coriscos-in-movement) by being (in another sense) always different in *logos* (being Coriscos-moving-through-P and then Coriscos-moving-through-P1).

We have seen also that earlier and later nows are the same in another way: *that, whatever it is, by being which they are* is the same. Each now divides the before and after in some change. It is because any now is a divider of a before and after in change that it is possible to count a single series of nows. Similarly, *that, whatever it is, by being*

ensures that there are no gaps in the change. In *Physics* IV, he says that time follows change. He cannot, then, appeal here to facts about the continuity of time to explain the unity of a change. Instead, he appeals to the sameness of the moving thing itself to explain the unity of the movement. An appeal to the *subject* of the motion could not provide this explanation. Hence, the need to introduce this odd entity, *the thing-in-motion*. This is, of course, a somewhat unsatisfactory answer to the problem, unless it can be shown that the sameness of the thing-in-motion does not itself depend on the sameness of the motion.

which the thing in motion is is always the same. For instance, Coriscos-in-motion-from-the-Lyceum-to-the-market remains that by being which it is, namely Coriscos. That there should be one subject of the movement (e.g. Coriscos) is a necessary condition for there being one movement. Hence, just as the sameness of *that by being which the now is* is a necessary condition for the unity of time, so also the sameness of *that by being which the thing-in-motion is* is a necessary condition for the unity of the movement.

PART V

TWO CONSEQUENCES OF ARISTOTLE'S ACCOUNT OF TIME

9

Being in Time

Aristotle uses the view of time that he has sketched to draw a distinction between things that are in time and things that are not ($220^b32–222^a9$, $222^b16–27$). The things that are in time, he claims, are all and only those that have a finite duration. Something that does not exist now can nevertheless be in time, so long as it exists for a limited length of time in the past or the future. The class of things that are not in time includes those things that never exist, but it also, more surprisingly, includes certain things that do exist. Anything that lasts forever exists without being in time ($221^b3–4$).

As we shall see, this notion of being in time falls out from his view that time is both a number and a measure of change. Something is in time, he says, just in case there is a time that is its number or, equivalently, its being is measured by time. The surprising claim that things that last forever are not in time is a consequence of this. If something lasts forever, there is no time that is its number (since we cannot count a now at which it begins and a now at which it ends) and its being cannot be measured by time (since it does not have a definite measurable duration) ($221^b4–5$).

But although it is presented as a consequence of his more general account of time, this claim that there are some things that are but are not in time is hard to reconcile with some of Aristotle's other views. At the very beginning of his account, he makes a strong assumption about time's universality. Time is, he says, 'both everywhere and with everything' (218^b13). That is one of the reasons why it cannot be a kind of change. But if there are some things that are but are not in time, how can time be 'everywhere and with everything'?

If this were the only difficulty, he might solve it by modifying his initial assumption about time's universality. There is, in any case, a passage in the *De Caelo* that implies that time is not, strictly speaking, universal. Aristotle argues there that things outside the heavens are not in time (or, for that matter in place), his reason being that time is a number of change, but nothing that was outside the heavens would be able to change.[1] However, in our passage from the *Physics*, he goes much further than this. His claim is not just about things that are 'outside the heavens'. He wants to say that *none* of the things that always exist is in time. What is puzzling about this is that, in an Aristotelian universe, some of the things that always exist are in constant motion. So he seems to be implying here that there are certain *changing things* that are not in time.

In the light of his other views about time, this is very surprising.[2] Whatever he thinks about the general claim that time is universal, he is committed at least to the more limited thesis that all changing things are part of the temporal order. Indeed, this thesis plays an important role in his account. We have seen that his view of the now implies that there is one now that is the now of all changes that are going on at it. And he goes to some lengths to show that time is a number of all continuous change, not just of this or that kind of change (223^a32–223^b1).[3] The claim that everlasting things are not in time threatens to undermine all this. The heavenly bodies last forever and yet are always in motion. How can something that undergoes constant circular motion fail to be in time?[4]

---

[1] The reason for claiming that nothing outside the heavens would be able to change, is that there can be no matter outside the heavens (since anything enmattered has a natural place in the universe) (*De Caelo* I.9.279^{a}11–22).

[2] Indeed, he appears straightforwardly to contradict the claim that certain changing things are not in time when he says, at 222^b30–1, that 'every alteration and every changing thing is in time'. The solution to this apparent contradiction is, I think, to distinguish between two senses of 'in time'. The sense in which all changing things are in time is that they are all part of the temporal order. But in the passages I discuss in this chapter, Aristotle is explaining a different sense in which something might be in time, and in *that* sense, things that change everlastingly are not in time. It is the purpose of this chapter to explain this other sense of *being in time*.

[3] Of course, the fact that an everlasting movement has no beginning or end implies that there is a *sense* in which it has no number. It is not possible to count all the way through it from beginning to end. But in another sense it does have a number, since any stage in the movement could be counted by counting the now that it was at.

[4] Admittedly, time's relationship to changes that go on forever is rather different from its relationship to other changes. Unlike other changes, those that go on forever do not have their own non-temporal before and after order. (See above, pp. 75–7). And the eternal rotary motion of the outermost sphere is, because of its regularity, uniquely suited to provide a unit for the measurement of time and of change. (See above, pp. 105–6.) But none

If we are to reconcile Aristotle's remarks about being in time with the rest of his account, we need to ask what exactly he means when he claims that everlasting things are not in time. Does he mean to deny that everlasting things stand in temporal relations to other things? Or is his point simply that if something lasts forever, it has neither a beginning nor an end in time (that is, there is neither a time before it began nor a time after it ceased)? The first of these alternatives would conflict with his views about the universality of time; the second threatens to make the claim that everlasting things are not in time trivially true, thus robbing it of any interest. I shall argue that Aristotle accepts neither alternative. On his view, everything that changes, whether or not it is in time, stands in temporal relations to other things. In that sense at least, time is universal.[5] But to say of some existing thing that it is not in time is to say more than that it has no beginning or end in time. Time is bound up with the being of those things that are *in time* in a way that it is not bound up with the being of those things that are not.

ARISTOTLE'S RESPONSE TO PLATO

The puzzle Aristotle faces is this. On the one hand, he claims that his account of time implies that things that don't begin or end in time are not in time. On the other hand, he is committed to the view that some of the things that don't begin or end in time are in everlasting motion. One response to this puzzle would be to distinguish between two ways in which something could lack a temporal beginning and end. Some things, like the heavenly bodies, do not begin or end in time because they persist for the whole of time; others lack a beginning or end because they are, in some sense, outside time. A distinction of this sort can be found in Plato. It will help us to understand Aristotle's discussion, if we can explain why he does not follow Plato's example in drawing such a distinction.

---

of this is enough to prepare us for the idea that things that are eternally changing are not in time at all.

[5] Aristotle's account of time does not, I think, provide us with enough evidence to settle whether or not he thinks that the 'things outside the heavens', which he mentions in *De Caelo* I.9, enter into temporal relations.

Plato's most extended discussion of time occurs in the *Timaeus*.[6] The *Timaeus* presents us with a creation myth. According to this myth, the universe was created using a certain model. The creator, or 'demiurge', modelled the universe on an unchanging and eternal living thing. For our purposes, an important aspect of this story is that *time* is created at a certain point. The demiurge creates time, together with the heavens, as a way of bringing order to the changing universe, thus making it as like as possible to the unchanging, eternal thing on which it is modelled. In describing the creation of time, Plato claims that 'was' and 'will be' are 'forms of time that have come to be' (37e). Though we mistakenly say that everlasting being is something that was and is and will be, we should, instead, say only that it 'is'.[7] This is because everlasting being cannot, in any sense, be said to become, whereas 'was' and 'will be' are properly said only of 'the becoming that passes in time' (38a).

It is not entirely clear what to make of this story about the creation of time.[8] But one thing that Plato seems to be doing here is drawing an implicit contrast between two different senses in which something might be everlasting (*aidios*). One sense of 'lasting forever' is *lasting for just as long as time does*. The heavens are everlasting in this sense; they were created along with time and they cannot be destroyed. The other

---

[6] *Timaeus* 37c–38e.

[7] The meaning of this claim depends on whether or not the 'is' that is correctly said of everlasting being is tenseless. If the 'is' is tenseless, then the claim is that everlasting being is neither past, present, nor future (so that it is wrong to say of it that it 'is now'). If the 'is' is present-tensed, then the claim is that everlasting being is always present: it always *is now* and never *was* nor *will be*. The latter interpretation seems to be more likely. Plato draws no distinction between the 'is' that is listed together with 'was' and 'will be' and the 'is' that is said of everlasting being. Moreover, at 38ª1–2 he says *only* that 'was' and 'will be' are 'properly said about the becoming that passes in time'. (Owen (1966) raises doubts about whether Plato is employing a fully tenseless 'is' here.)

[8] One question that is often asked is whether the story is meant to be taken literally. There was an ancient view, attributed by the Greek commentators to Xenocrates, that the *Timaeus* creation story could be explanatory without being literally true (see Vlastos 1965a: 383, n. 1). Aristotle considers and rejects this view at *De Caelo* I.10.279ᵇ32–280ª10. He makes it quite clear that he thinks Plato holds that time is created. At *Physics* VIII.1, he says: 'Plato alone holds that time is created, saying that it is simultaneous with the world, and that the world came into being' (251ᵇ17–19). Vlastos (1956: 412–14) also argues that Plato's claim that time has a beginning should be taken literally, but he points out that for Plato, time is essentially measurable. The claim that *measurable time* only began when the heavens were created is, he implies, less bizarre than the claim that things were not even temporally ordered before the creation of the heavens.

sense of 'lasting forever' is *having no beginning or end at all*. The eternal
living thing on which the universe is modelled is everlasting in this
second sense;[9] it is neither generable nor destructible.

Because he has the resources to make this distinction, Plato is in a
position to claim that things that are everlasting in the former sense are
in time in a way that things that are everlasting in the latter sense are
not.[10] The heavenly bodies last throughout time and engage in constant
motion. Each year they have a past that is a year longer. We can say of
them not just that they are, but also that they were and will be. In
contrast, the eternal living thing, which exists everlastingly without
beginning or end, is not subject to any kind of change. Since it has no
beginning, it cannot even be said to accumulate, as the years go by, a
longer and longer past.[11] It *is*, but it never was nor will be. In this sense,
it is outside time.

Aristotle, like Plato, thinks that things that exist everlastingly without
beginning or end are, in a certain sense, not in time. As we shall see, he,
like Plato, is swayed by the thought that things that have no beginning
do not, as time goes by, accumulate a longer and longer past.[12] But for
Aristotle, the class of such things is much broader than it is for Plato.
This is because Aristotle rejects one of the basic presuppositions of
Plato's account. He rejects the view that time has a beginning.[13] If
time itself has no beginning, then there is no distinction between things
that last for just as long as time does and things that have no beginning
at all: anything that lasts throughout time is beginningless. It follows *a
fortiori* that anything that has been moving for all time must be
beginningless. This is why Aristotle, unlike Plato, is committed to the
view that the heavenly bodies are not in time.

Because of this, Aristotle must also reject Plato's view of what it is to
be in time. He must, that is, reject the view that we can only say 'was'
and 'will be' of things that are in time. According to Aristotle, the fact
that the heavenly bodies move implies that they stand in temporal

---

[9] Plato calls it 'everlasting' (*aidios*) at *Timaeus* 37d1.
[10] He does not use the expression 'in time' here, but he clearly does mean to
distinguish between the way in which things of these two different kinds are related
to time.
[11] It cannot be 'growing older or younger by the lapse of time' (*Timaeus* 38a). For an
explanation of the addition, 'or younger', see n. 27, below.
[12] They do not, that is, grow older. See below, p. 154.
[13] For the argument that time cannot have a beginning, see above, Ch. 4, n. 29.

relations to other things. Moreover, on his account, there is an important connection between standing in temporal relations and being past, present, and future: something can only stand in temporal relations if it itself either is, or is divisible into parts that are, successively future, present, and past. That this is so is an interesting consequence of the role he assigns the series of nows in determining temporal order. As we have already seen, to stand in temporal relations is to be ordered by a series of nows that we count when we count the before and after in changes. In counting a now, we make a division in everything that is at the now. Hence, everything that is temporally ordered and is not instantaneous can be divided at a now into a part that is before the now (and hence past) and a part that is after the now (and hence future). Anything that stands in temporal relations is (or at least has parts that are) successively future, present, and past.[14]

I have argued that Aristotle cannot accept Plato's view of what it is to be in time. One might expect, then, that his account of being in time would contain some direct argument against this view. But in fact, for the most part he just assumes that it is false. There is only one place here where he seems to have Plato's view of being in time as his target. This is in his discussion of the claim that 'being in time' is equivalent to 'being when time is'.[15] He is at some pains to emphasize that this claim is mistaken. 'It is clear' he says 'that to be in time is not to be when time is' (221ª19–20). His insistence on this point can seem rather odd. Why does he think that this, in particular, is a claim worth refuting? The answer, I want to suggest, is that he is using the expression 'being when time is' to mean *being successively future, present, and past.*

Some evidence that 'being when time is' should be understood in this way is provided by Plato's use of a similar expression in one of the arguments in the second half of the *Parmenides.* This argument defends the view that anything that is must partake of time. It does so by claiming that anything that is must be 'together with time'. Parmenides asks, 'Is not *to be* partaking of being with time present, just as *was* is communion of being together with time past and, in turn, *will be* is communion of being together with time future?' (*Parmenides,*

---

[14] It would be possible to have an account of time on which this was not so. One such account is given by Hugh Mellor, who claims that there are real temporal relations of before and after, but denies that anything is really past, present, or future (Mellor 1998).
[15] *Physics* IV.12.221ª19–26.

151e–152a). This notion of *being together with time* is very close in meaning to Aristotle's 'being when time is'. When he writes of 'being when time is', Aristotle means, I think, *being together with present, future, and past time*. Those things that 'are when time is' are just those of which it is true to say 'is' (at some time) and 'was' or 'will be' (at others).[16]

Aristotle argues that to treat the notion of *being in time* as if it were just equivalent to *being when time is* is to rob the notion of its significance. While it is true that if something is in time then it is when time is, this truth does not capture anything important about the essential relationship between time and those things that are in time. To *be when time is* is simply to be simultaneous with other things. But the fact that something stands in this or that relation of simultaneity does not reveal anything about the *kind* of thing it is. In general, he claims, the notion of simultaneity is too weak to capture what we mean when we say that one thing is in another. To be in place, for instance, is not to be when place is. [17] The right account of being in time, Aristotle assumes, must reveal some essential difference between those things that are in time and those that are not. The fact that those things that are in time are when time is tells us nothing about the essential nature of such things. In that sense, it is merely an accidental fact about them ($221^a23–4$).[18]

Aristotle's argument here involves something of a sleight of hand. Whether a thing stands in this or that relation of simultaneity may not reveal anything significant about its nature, but whether it stands in any relations of simultaneity at all surely does. I have argued that, as Aristotle is using the expression, the things that are 'when time is' are just those of which we can at different times say 'was', 'is', and 'will be'

[16] As I have already said, there is reason to think that Plato's view in the *Timaeus* is that everlasting being is always present, rather than that it is neither past, present, nor future. If this is right, then Plato's own answer to the argument in the *Parmenides* would be that something that partakes of being can be present, without ever being either past or future (and hence without 'partaking in time', if that implies being together not only with present time, but also with past and future time). Aristotle does not show any sensitivity to the distinction between the claim that things that are not in time are always present and the claim that such things are neither past, present, nor future. (He does not, for instance, consider the view that things that are not in time might *be when present time is*, without ever being past or future.) But that should not surprise us. On his account, both claims are equally mistaken.

[17] Indeed, he says, if it were generally true that for x to be in y was for x to be when y was, then the fact that a grain of millet existed simultaneously with the heaven would be a reason for concluding that the heaven was in the grain of millet ($221^a21–3$).

[18] For my understanding of this passage, I am indebted to Hussey (1993: 165).

(and that these are, on his view, just those things that enter into temporal relations). The view that there is an important distinction between things of this kind and things that only 'are' cannot be dismissed simply by appealing, as he does in this passage, to general considerations about the significance of particular relations of simultaneity.

However, the rest of Aristotle's account of time does provide some support for the point he is making here. According to this account, *everything that is* is when time is. That is to say, everything that is enters into temporal relations and is (or at least has parts that are) successively future, present, and past.[19] This suggests that *being when time is* is not a matter of being related to time in any specially significant way.

Aristotle wants to claim that among the things that are when time is there is a class of things that stand in a special relationship to time: their being is, in a sense still to be explained, bound up with the being of time. His account of being in time is designed to distinguish *these* things from everything else. To understand what is special about the way in which these things are related to time, we need to look more closely at Aristotle's positive characterization of being in time.

THE TWO CRITERIA FOR BEING IN TIME

When Aristotle says that those things that have a finite duration are just those things that are 'in time', he is not simply telling us how he proposes to use the expression 'in time'. He is making a substantive claim about the way in which things that have a finite duration are related to time. So, at least, I shall argue.

But what exactly is he claiming about such things when he says that they alone are 'in time'? As we have seen, he does not think that they are the only things that stand in temporal relations. Nor does he want to say that they are the only things that can be past, present, or future. On his view, they are not even the only things that are capable of movement. All

---

[19] The only possible exceptions to this general claim are the 'things outside the heavens', mentioned in *De Caelo* I.9.279^{a}11–22 (see n. 144 above). Aristotle may be suggesting, in the *De Caelo*, that such things are outside time in a more radical sense (e.g. that they do not stand in temporal relations at all). But if so, he makes no mention of this in our chapters of the *Physics*.

this raises questions about the significance of the distinction between being in time and not being in time. What is special about the way in which things that have a finite duration are related to time? What are Aristotle's grounds for thinking that such things are, in an important sense, different *in kind* from everything else? In the remainder of this chapter, I shall attempt to answer these questions. I shall look first at Aristotle's account of the two criteria for being in time and then turn to his discussion of the odd idea that time is a kind of cause.

Aristotle lays out two different criteria for distinguishing between things that are in time and things that are not. Each of them draws attention to a connection between his notion of being in time and his overall account. The first criterion draws on the fact that time is a number, the second, on the fact that it is a measure.

The criterion that appeals to time's being a number equates being in time with being surrounded by time (221^a16–18). Something is surrounded by time just in case there is time before and after it. This way of understanding what it is to be in time corresponds to one sense of the expression 'in number'.[20] A group of things is said to be in number because there is a number of them. For instance, a collection of seven sheep is in number because there are seven of them. Things that are in number in this way are, in a certain sense, 'surrounded by number'. There is a number of sheep that is greater than the seven and a number that is less. Analogously, if something is 'in time', then there is a time of it (that is, a period of time during which it is) and there are other times that are earlier and later than this time. Given Aristotle's view that time itself has no beginning or end, those things that are surrounded by time are just those things that have a finite duration.[21] By itself, then, this criterion tells us only that the things that are in time are just those that last for a finite length of time. It does not help us to understand what it

[20] Aristotle points out that there is also another sense in which we use the expression 'in number' and that this corresponds to a different sense in which something can be in time. One way to be in number is to be an aspect of number (for instance, a part or a property of number). The unit and the odd and the even are in number in this sense. Correspondingly, some things are 'in time' in the sense that they are aspects of time. The now is in time in the way that the unit is in number. The before and after are in time in the way that the odd and the even are in number (221^a11–16).

[21] If time itself had a beginning or an end, then something might have a finite duration without being surrounded by time. Something might, for instance, begin when time began and then only last for a finite length of time.

is that we are saying about such things when we claim that they alone are in time.

Can the second criterion provide us with a richer understanding of being in time? According to this second criterion, a thing is in time if and only if its being is measured by time. Things that always are, for instance, are not in time because 'their being (*einai*) is not measured by time' (221^{b}5). This stands in need of some explanation. What is it for something's *being* to be measured by time? And what are Aristotle's grounds for supposing that the things that have their being measured by time will be precisely those that have a finite duration?

He says that the things of which time measures the being 'have their being in being at rest or changing' (221^{b}27–8). I take this to mean that it is part of the nature (or being) of such things that they change and are at rest. This suggests that the claim that time measures their *being* is the claim that it measures this thing that is essential to their being. It measures the period for which they are changing and/or at rest (rather than, for instance, measuring the period for which they are of a certain weight or bulk).

Time will measure the thing that is changing and the thing that is at rest, the one in so far as it is changing and the other in so far as it is at rest; for it will measure their change and their rest, [measuring] how great each is. Hence, the changing thing will not be measurable by time simply in so far as it is of some quantity, but in so far as its change is of some quantity.   (221^{b}16–20)

On Aristotle's view, something that is at rest is something that has the capacity to change but is not changing.[22] Hence, things that have their being in changing or resting are just those things that, by their nature, have the capacity to change.

Does this, then, provide an answer to our question about how things that are in time differ in kind from things that are not? Is *having their being in changing and resting* what distinguishes things that are in time from everything else? Unfortunately not. On Aristotle's view, the heavenly bodies, though they are not in time, are essentially such as to move. His reason for denying that time measures the being of such things must be that it cannot measure the *total* period for which they are changing.

---

[22] An unchanging thing only counts as being at rest if it is capable of changing (221^{b}12–14). A number, for instance, is not the sort of thing that can be at rest.

But the reason for *this* is simply that there *is* no total period for which they are changing: the heavenly bodies are in everlasting movement. This does not, in itself, show that they differ in some further way from things that are in time. It provides us with no reason to suppose that the distinction between things that are in time and things that are not amounts to anything more than the distinction between things that exist for a finite (and only a finite) length of time and things that do not.

Aristotle's two criteria both identify the same things as 'in time'. On both, something that lasts for a finite length of time must be in time. For example, a thing that is wholly past, like Homer, is in time (221^{b}31–222^{a}2). There was time before Homer existed and time after he existed, so he is surrounded by time. Moreover, he is, by his very nature, such as to change or be at rest, and the total period of his changing or being at rest is a measurable period of time; that is, his *being* is measured by time. The two criteria both imply that things that never are are not in time. Aristotle's example of such a thing is *the diagonal's being commensurable with the side* (222^{a}6).[23] There is no time before or after *the diagonal's being commensurable with the side*, nor is *the being of the diagonal's commensurability with the side* something that can be measured by time. Likewise, things that always exist 'considered as such, are not in time, for they are not surrounded by time, nor is their being measured by time' (221^{b}3–5).

The two criteria lay out very clearly the connection between Aristotle's use of the expression 'being in time' and his view that time is a number and a measure. Neither of them, though, sheds much light on our question about the *significance* of the claim that everlasting things are not in time. We are still left wondering why Aristotle thinks that the distinction between things that are in time and things that are not is of such importance. An answer to this question is suggested by some remarks he makes about the idea that time is a kind of cause.

---

[23] His use of this example suggests that his distinction between things that are in time and things that are not is meant to apply not just to objects (such as Homer) but also to (what we would call) states of affairs (though presumably his distinction between things that *get older* in time and things that do not is a distinction between different kinds of object).

TIME AS A CAUSE

When he is spelling out the notion of being in time, Aristotle makes the puzzling claim that time is a kind of cause. [24] It causes the things that are in time to get old and ultimately to cease to be.

He holds that the things that grow older and cease to be are just those that are in time. [25] The claim that things that are in time eventually cease to be is uncontroversial. As we have seen, all such things last for a finite length of time. Conversely, things that are not in time are everlasting, so clearly they never cease to be. [26] The claim that the things that *get older* are just those that are in time requires some explanation. [27] One way in which a thing can be said to *get older* is that it *accumulates more years in its past*. Something that lasts forever does not, in this sense, get any older, since it always has an infinite past: the length of time for which it has existed is not any greater this year than it was last year. [28] In contrast, anything that has a finite duration has, each year that it continues to exist, a past that is one year longer. Another sense in which we might say that something gets older is that it ages physically: it accumulates not

---

[24] *Physics* IV.12.221^{a}30–^{b}7 and 13.222^{b}16–27.

[25] He claims that growing older and ceasing to be are the effects of time (221^{a}30–^{b}2) and he implies that all and only things that are in time are affected by time (221^{b}5–7).

[26] Aristotle's discussion of being in time assumes that anything that exists must either have a finite duration or last forever without beginning or end. He is assuming, then, that it is impossible for anything to have come to be but never cease to be, or conversely, to cease to be without ever having come to be. This is a view he defends in *De Caelo* I.10–12. There is little agreement among interpreters about what exactly his arguments for it are. These chapters in the *De Caelo* are helpfully discussed by Broadie (1982b, especially ch. 4), Judson (1983), Sorabji (1983: 277–9), and Leggatt (1995: 213–21).

[27] It recalls a claim made in Plato's *Parmenides*, where it is said that the things that are in time become older and younger than themselves and that they differ, in this respect, from things that are not in time (*Parmenides*, 141a–d). Aristotle rejects the odd claim that things that are in time become younger as well as older (221^{b}1). The thought behind this claim in the *Parmenides* seems to be that if *x* becomes older than *y*, *y* must become younger than *x*. This is taken to imply that if something becomes older than itself, it must also become younger than itself (on the grounds that if *x* becomes older than *x*, *x* must also become younger than *x*).

[28] As I explained above (p. 147), in this, Aristotle differs importantly from Plato. On Plato's view, something can last for the whole of time without having an infinite past (since, on this view, time has a beginning). So for Plato (unlike Aristotle), it is possible for something to last for the whole of time and yet have, each year, a past that is one year longer.

just years but also grey hairs and wrinkles. To get older, in this sense, is to be subject to a gradual process of decay.[29] Something that lasts for an infinite length of time cannot age in this sense either: if it had been decaying for an infinitely long time it would already have fully decayed. On the other hand, anything that has only a finite duration must, Aristotle thinks, be the sort of thing that decays. He holds that something that has a finite duration must be essentially such as to have a finite duration. If it is not brought to an untimely end by external interference, such a thing will cease to be of itself.[30] The process that leads up to its ceasing to be is a process of natural decay.

Aristotle's view is that degenerative changes, such as growing older and ceasing to be, are caused by time. Moreover, he claims, time is directly responsible *only* for changes of this sort.[31] In support of this latter claim, he invokes some of our ordinary assumptions about time.[32] We tend to think, he says, that time is responsible for degenerative change but not for coming to be. We think this because degenerative change, unlike coming-to-be, seems not to need an external cause (222^{b}22–4). When we see a change occurring without an apparent external cause, we assume that it is caused by time (222^{b}24–5). This assumption is reflected in our everyday speech. We say 'time wears things away' and 'everything grows old through time' and 'forgets through time', but we do not say that time is responsible for getting younger, becoming beautiful or learning (221^{a}30–^{b}2). As I explained in

---

[29] In the *Generation of Animals*, Aristotle says that old age is rightly thought of as a natural disease, and disease as acquired old age (since some diseases produce effects that are characteristic of old age, such as grey hairs) (V.4.784^{b}32–4).

[30] Anything that in fact has a finite duration is something that has come to be, but Aristotle argues that anything that has come to be must eventually cease to be (*De Caelo* I.12). (For discussion of his argument see again the references in n. 26.) The fact that such a thing eventually ceases to be cannot, then, just be an accident. Hence, *having a finite duration* cannot be an accidental feature of a thing. As I shall explain, there is some reason to think that he is also committed to the stronger claim that anything that has a finite duration is essentially such as to exist for a certain definite *amount* of time (p. 156).

[31] He says that though time 'in itself' is a cause of ceasing to be, it is accidentally also a cause of coming to be and of being (222^{b}20–2), presumably because the ceasing to be of one thing is accidentally the coming to be of another. For example, the ceasing to be of this piece of wood (when I burn it) is also the coming to be of this pile of ashes.

[32] He also claims, rather unconvincingly, that his definition of time explains the fact that time is responsible only for degenerative change. The explanation is that time is 'a number of change and change removes what is present' (221^{b}1–3). But this explanation is open to an obvious objection, as it is equally true that change adds what is not present.

Chapter 2, according to Aristotle, it is at least prima facie reasonable to suppose that ordinary assumptions of this sort are true.[33] But what does he mean when he says that time is a *cause* of these changes? At one point he suggests that things that are in time are *acted upon* by time (221^a30). This is an idea he later rejects. Though time is a cause, it is not an agent: it does not produce (*poiei*) the changes that it causes (222^b25–7). Nevertheless, the claim that time is a cause of *any* kind is an odd claim for him to be making. He has defined time as a number of change. But if time is by definition something we count by counting changes, how can it be the cause of some of these changes?

To answer this question, it is necessary to remember that Aristotle's notion of cause is broader than ours.[34] One of the Aristotelian types of cause is the formal cause. We cite the formal cause of a thing when we explain how it is by referring to its essence. For instance, Aristotle says that the ratio of two to one is the formal cause of the octave (194^b26–8). Time, I want to suggest, is a kind of formal cause. More precisely, it is part of the formal cause of a thing's natural decay.[35]

This view depends on the idea that lasting for a certain definite time-span is built into the essence of things that are in time. In the case of living things, at least, this is quite plausible. Living for about ten to fifteen years is just part of what it is to be a dog. Aristotle discusses the reasons for differences in life-span in his treatise, *On Length and Shortness of Life*. Molluscs, he says, live for only a year. The longest-lived animals are sanguineous land animals, such as humans and elephants. But the longest-lived of all things are certain kinds of plant, such as the date palm.[36]

The natural life-span of a living creature is part of the creature's nature. It is the source of some of its natural changes. For instance, it is because it has, by nature, such a life-span that the creature will start to decay when it reaches a certain age.[37] That is not to say that old age explains a death in the sense that a stroke or a heart attack does. The

---

[33] See above p. 38.

[34] For Aristotle's account of causation, see *Physics* II.3.

[35] It is interesting to compare here Ben Morison's discussion of the sense in which place, for Aristotle, has a kind of power (*dunamis*). Places, Morison claims, are 'parts of . . . the formal causes of the elements' (2002: 53).

[36] *On Length and Shortness of Life*, 4.

[37] Aristotle criticizes Democritus' account of respiration on the grounds that it does not explain why all animals must die at some time, 'not, however, at any chance time, but

difference between the two types of explanation is simply the difference between an explanation in terms of the formal cause and an explanation in terms of material processes. That a creature will naturally live only for a certain length of time is determined by its form: by the fact that it is, for instance, a mollusc rather than a man. The precise manner in which it dies depends on facts about its circumstances and its material makeup.[38] When something ages naturally towards the end of its life, its expected life-span is part of the formal cause of this ageing.

These considerations give some sense to the idea that time can be a kind of cause. They help us to understand what Aristotle might mean by his claim that all and only those things that are in time are affected by time. This claim has an important place in his discussion of being in time. It provides him with an answer to our question about the significance of the distinction between things that are in time and things that are not. The answer is that time's relation to things that are in time is importantly different from its relation to other things. Though something is in time just in case it has a finite duration, being in time amounts to more than having a finite duration. To be in time is to be something that is, in the sense we have explained, affected by time.

But is this a claim that Aristotle has the resources to defend? I shall end by noting a point on which he seems especially vulnerable to criticism. On the interpretation I have given, it is essential to his view that anything that has a finite duration lasts, by nature, for a certain particular time span. That is why time counts as part of the formal cause of the decay of anything that is in time. But, although this is a plausible claim about *living things*, it is not clear what grounds there could be for saying that it is true of *everything* that has a finite duration. Even if we are convinced by Aristotle's view that anything that comes to be must at some point cease to be,[39] it requires further argument to establish that

when natural owing to old age and, when unnatural to violence' (*On Youth, Old Age, Life and Death, and Respiration*, 10(4).472ª16–18).

[38] Aristotle holds that an animal's death is always caused in some way by lack of heat. When the animal gets old, it ceases to be able to keep its internal fire cool and this fire goes out from exhaustion. Natural death is 'the exhaustion of the heat owing to lapse of time (*dia chronou mēkos*), and occurring at the end of life. In plants, this is called withering, in animals, death. Death, in old age, is the exhaustion of the organ due to its inability, on account of old age, to cause refrigeration' (*On Youth, Old Age, Life and Death, and Respiration*, 24(18).479ᵇ1–5).

[39] A view that (as I have said) he defends at length in *De Caelo* I.10–12.

anything that ceases to be must be something that, by nature, lasts for a certain definite time span. Unless Aristotle can show this, then he has only established that *living* things are related to time in a distinctive way (since time is part of the formal cause of some of their natural changes). To be sure, this in itself is an interesting claim. But it does not on its own support the distinction he wants to draw between things that are in time and things that are not. For it does not indicate any special way in which all and only those things that have a finite duration are related to time.

10

Time and the Soul

Given that time is by definition something countable, the question naturally arises whether its existence depends on the existence of beings, like ourselves, who can count it. Aristotle raises this question towards the end of his discussion (223ᵃ21–9). Someone might be puzzled, he says, about whether there could be time if there were no ensouled beings. He presents an argument that there could not be.

The argument is that since time is a kind of number, it is necessarily countable. As such, it can only exist in a world in which there are beings that can count. Since the only beings that can count are beings that have intellective souls, there can only be time in a world in which there are such beings.[1] He goes on to point out that this argument gives us no reason to think that *change* depends on the soul, since change, though it is closely connected to time, is not something that is necessarily countable:

Someone might raise the puzzle whether if there were no soul there would be time or not. For if it is impossible for there to be something to do the counting, it is impossible also that anything should be countable, so that it is clear that there will not be number. For number is either the counted or the countable. But if nothing else has the nature to count than soul (and in the soul, the intellect), it is impossible for there to be time if there is no soul, except that[2] there could be that, whatever it is, by being which time is (*touto ho pote on estin ho chronos*), for example, if it is possible for there to be change without soul. The before and after are in change and time is these in so far as they are countable. (223ᵃ21–9)[3]

---

[1] On Aristotle's view, human beings are the only animals that have intellect (that is, *nous*). But to say that time depends for its existence on intellective souls is not *necessarily* to say that it depends for its existence on humans. Aristotle thinks that god is a kind of intellect.

[2] The Greek is '*all' ē*'. It could also be translated: 'but in fact . . . '.

[3] It is not clear whether Aristotle is saying here that the before and after in change would exist (but not be countable) in a world without ensouled beings or simply that change would exist in such a world. That is, it is not clear whether *touto ho pote on estin ho chronos* refers to change or to the before and after in change.

We are already familiar with Aristotle's view that time is necessarily countable. But nevertheless the argument he presents here is puzzling. Why should we accept, for instance, that something countable could only exist in a world in which there were beings able to count? Does Aristotle himself really believe this? Time, as we have seen, is the universal before and after order within which all changes are arranged. Does Aristotle really think that, in the absence of beings able to count, changes would not be arranged in such an order? Still more puzzling is the suggestion that time depends on the soul in a way in which change does not. This seems to imply that there could be a world in which there was change but no time. But Aristotle has already argued that there can be no change without time. He says that 'it is manifest that every alteration and every changing thing is in time' (222^b30-1).[4]

One way in which commentators have responded to these puzzles has been to put forward an alternative interpretation.[5] According to this interpretation, Aristotle does not himself endorse the conclusion that time depends on the soul. Instead, he expects the reader to see that the argument he presents for this conclusion is flawed. Proponents of this interpretation think that he makes this clear when he goes on to say that there could be change in a world without ensouled beings, that is, when he adds: 'except that there could be that, whatever it is, by being which time is, for example, if it is possible for there to be change without soul'. On this interpretation, Aristotle is expecting us to draw the conclusion that since there can be change in a world without souls, there can be time in such a world too.[6]

I shall argue that it is a mistake to resort to this alternative interpretation here. Once we fully understand Aristotle's view about the way in which time is countable, we should be able to see for ourselves not just that it is mind-dependent but also that it is mind-dependent in a way in which change is not.

---

[4] As we saw in the last chapter, there is, though, a sense in which changes that go on forever are not in time.

[5] Aquinas *In Phys.* Lecture 23, 629. And, in modern times: Festugière (1934), Dubois (1967), Goldschmidt (1982).

[6] Note that for this alternative interpretation to be plausible, there would have to be an *obvious* flaw in the argument Aristotle presents, since he himself does not draw our attention to any such flaw. Moreover, it would have to be obvious that the claim that there could be change in a world without ensouled beings implied that there could be time in such a world too, since Aristotle (on this interpretation) leaves it to the reader to draw this conclusion.

THE CLAIM THAT TIME DEPENDS
ON ENSOULED BEINGS IN A WAY
IN WHICH CHANGE DOES NOT

Aristotle says that if there were no ensouled beings, there could be no time, but there might nevertheless be change. But he also thinks that there can be no change without time (222^{b}30–1). The key to understanding how these views can be consistent lies in the interpretation of the two counterfactuals:

if there were no souls, there would be no time;
if there were no souls, there might be changes.

For a modern reader, it is natural to read these using the language of possible worlds:

in any possible world in which there are no ensouled beings, there is no time;
in some of the possible worlds in which there are no ensouled beings, there is change.

If this is how we are to understand the counterfactuals, then they straightforwardly imply that there are possible worlds in which there is change but no time.

A clue that this is not the right way to understand them is that Aristotle has the (to us rather strange) view that it is impossible for there to be a world without ensouled beings. He thinks that there always have been and will be beings with souls, and that this implies that it is necessary that there are such beings.[7] Thus, when he asks whether there could be time or change in a world without ensouled beings, he is not envisioning a way the world *might have been*, and asking whether there would be time or change in a world like that.

How then should we understand the claim that in a world without ensouled beings there might be change but no time? It is, I think, a claim about the essential natures of time and of change. On Aristotle's view, the relation between time and the soul is importantly different

---

[7] According to Aristotle, what exists eternally, exists necessarily. (See, for example, *Generation and Corruption* II.11.338^{a}1–3, *Metaphysics* XIV.2, 1088^{b}23–4, *De Caelo* I.12.)

from the relation between change and the soul. Since time, change, and the soul all exist in every possible world, this difference cannot be captured by talk of what is true in other possible worlds. The difference is this. The nature of time itself implies that time cannot exist in the absence of ensouled beings. On the other hand, it does not follow *simply from the nature of change* that there could not be change without time, and it also does not follow from the nature of change that change could not exist in the absence of ensouled beings. The nature of a thing is expressed in its definition. Aristotle defines time as 'a number of change in respect of the before and after'. From this definition, it follows that time could not exist in the absence of ensouled beings. He defines change in terms of potentiality.[8] This definition alone does not imply that change could only exist in a world in which there were such beings.[9]

Note that for all I have said, Aristotle might hold that there is some *other* reason to think that there can only be change if there are souls.[10] He is very noncommittal about whether in a world without souls there could in fact be change. He says only: 'for example, if it is possible for there to be change without soul' (223^a27–8). If my interpretation is right, it is not surprising that he feels no need here to settle whether or not this really is possible. For although he asks what would be true if there were no ensouled beings, his primary interest is not in exploring what the world would be like if, *per impossibile*, there were no such beings; he is simply using this question as a device by which to clarify certain facts about the relation between the nature of change and the nature of time.

We can now see that the claim that time depends on the soul in a way in which change does not is consistent with the claim that there can be no change without time. Since it is necessary that there is both time and change, there will be time in every possible world in which there is change. (In *that* sense, the existence of change is a sufficient condition for the existence of time.) But it does not follow simply from the nature

---

[8] *Physics* III.1–2. I explain Aristotle's account of change in the Introduction.

[9] This idea that something can be necessary in virtue of the definition of X, but not in virtue of the definition of Y is something I have already discussed. See above, Ch. 2, p. 33. For a modern defence of this idea see Fine (1994).

[10] As Simplicius says (*In Phys.* 760), perhaps the cyclic motion of the heavens has to be caused by some intelligence (and other changes cannot occur without this one). Simplicius rightly says that whether or not this is so makes no difference to Aristotle's argument here.

of change that a world in which there is change will be a world in which there is time (as it does follow from the nature of change that a world in which there is change will be a world in which there is potentiality).[11] That there is time follows from the fact that there is change together with the fact that this change is countable.

THE ARGUMENT THAT IF THERE WERE NO ENSOULED BEINGS, THERE WOULD BE NO TIME

We have seen how Aristotle can consistently claim that time depends on the soul in a way in which change does not. We now need to look in more detail at the argument that he presents. Let us remind ourselves of what he says:

> if it is impossible for there to be something to do the counting, it is impossible also that anything should be countable, so that it is clear that there will not be number. For number is either the counted or the countable. But if nothing else has the nature to count than soul (and in the soul, the intellect), it is impossible for there to be time if there is no soul ... (*Physics* D 14, 223ª21–6)

The argument seems to be:

(i) Time is a kind of number, and is therefore something either counted or countable (223ª24–5 and definition of time at 219ᵇ1–2).

(ii) Beings with intellective souls are the only things able to count (223ª25–6: 'if nothing else has the nature to count ... ').

(iii) If it is impossible for there to be something that is able to count, then it is impossible for there to be anything countable (or counted) (223ª22–4).

---

[11] That Aristotle doesn't think it just absurd to suppose that there might be change but no time is suggested, I think, by his response to the creation story in Plato's *Timaeus*. As we have already seen, Aristotle takes this story literally (see Ch. 9, n. 8). He thinks that, on Plato's view, time was created along with the heavens (*Physics* 251ᵇ17–19). As Aristotle says in the *Metaphysics*, Plato also held that there was a kind of motion even before the creation of the heavens (XII.6.1071ᵇ31–1072ª2). Though Aristotle argues against these views, he never makes what to us would seem the obvious objection. He never says that Plato must be wrong since his account implies that before the creation of the heavens there was motion but there was no time.

Therefore: (iv) if there is nothing able to count, then there can be no
time (iii and i).

Therefore: (v) if there are no ensouled beings, then there can be no
time (ii and iv). (This conclusion is drawn on line 223ª26.)

It is important to appreciate that this is really just the *sketch* of an
argument. If we are to understand it, we need to ask not just whether
it is sound as it stands, but also whether it would be sound, if its
premisses were supplemented with other things Aristotle believed.
Bearing this in mind will help us to answer one of the main objections
that has been brought against the argument.

MIGNUCCI'S OBJECTION—THE DROPPING OF 'IMPOSSIBLE'

Mario Mignucci has claimed that the argument is invalid. Its premisses
do not entail that in a world without ensouled beings, there could be no
time. They entail only the weaker conclusion: in a world in which it was
impossible for there to be ensouled beings, there could be no time.[12]

Mignucci argues as follows. In my premiss (iii) (lines 223ª22–4),
Aristotle says that if it is impossible for there to be something that is able
to count, then it is impossible for there to be anything countable. It does
not follow from this that if there is nothing able to count, then there can
be no time (my iv). All that follows is that if it is *impossible* for there to
be anything that is able to count, then it is impossible for there to be
time. From this, Aristotle should conclude only that if it is *impossible* for
there to be souls, it is impossible for there to be time. He is not entitled
to draw the stronger conclusion that if there *are* no souls, there can be
no time.[13]

---

[12] Mignucci (1984: 175–211).

[13] According to Mignucci, if Aristotle had really meant to endorse the stronger claim
(that there can be no time in a world without souls), then he would have been making a
simple logical mistake. Mignucci claims that Aristotle would not make a mistake of this
sort. He concludes that Aristotle cannot have thought that this argument proved that
there could be no time in a world without souls. Mignucci himself does not adopt the
traditional realist view that Aristotle here is presenting an argument he believes to be
fallacious. Instead, Mignucci thinks that Aristotle is in fact arguing for the weaker
conclusion (that if it is impossible for there to be souls, it is impossible for there to be
time) and has expressed himself carelessly here.

Mignucci is, of course, right about the logic of the argument as Aristotle presents it here. However, he is wrong to say that Aristotle is only entitled to the weaker conclusion. On Aristotle's view, the weaker conclusion implies the stronger. The ability to count is an ability that a thing has in virtue of having an intellective soul. But to have an intellective soul is to be a member of some kind that, if it exists, exists eternally.[14] Hence, if there were ever a time at which nothing was able to count, then there would never be anything able to count. But according to Aristotle, a world in which there was never anything able to count would be a world in which it was impossible for there to be anything able to count.

This last claim contradicts the natural assumption that the world might simply have *happened* not to contain beings that were able to count. Aristotle is committed to denying this assumption because of his views about necessity. He holds quite generally that if nothing of a certain kind ever is, then nothing of that kind could possibly be. Indeed, he makes this claim (though in a rather convoluted way) in an earlier section of his account of time. He says, in *Physics* IV.12, that 'all and only those things (*hosōn*) of which the opposite not always is are capable of being and not being' (222^{a}7–8).[15] An example of something whose opposite 'not always is' is *Socrates' sitting*. (*Socrates' not sitting* is something that not always is, since it is sometimes true that Socrates is

---

[14] He thinks that species are not the sort of things that can come into or go out of existence. *Generation of Animals* II.1.731^{b}24–732^{a}1, *De Anima* II.4.415^{a}25–^{b}7. If an *animal* has an intellective soul then it is a member of the human species. The only other kind of intellect intellective soul is god, and it, obviously, exists eternally if it exists at all.

[15] I refer to *Physics* IV.12 here because this is a passage from Aristotle's discussion of time. But the conclusion that if souls never existed it would be impossible for them to exist also follows from a certain form of the principle of plenitude. Sorabji (1980: 128–37) has argued that Aristotle holds that a thing cannot *always* be possible without at some time being actual. (For example, Aristotle assumes that if the stars had the capacity to stop moving, they would, since they exist forever, eventually exercise this capacity, *Metaphysics* IX.8.1050^{b}20–8.) If Aristotle does indeed subscribe to this general principle, then he is committed to the view that (1) if it is always possible for there to be souls, then at some time there will be souls. But Aristotle also holds that (2) if it is ever possible for there to be souls, it will always be possible for there to be souls. Having a soul of a certain kind is essential to being a member of this or that species, and a species, if it exists, exists eternally. (This, at least, is Aristotle's view. See previous footnote.) The existence of ensouled beings is not, then, the kind of thing that can be possible at one time and impossible at another. From (1) and (2), it follows that if it is ever possible for there to be souls, then there will at some time be souls. And from this it follows that if there are never any souls, it is impossible for there to be souls.

sitting.) By contrast, *the diagonal's being commensurable* is something whose opposite always is (since it is never true that the diagonal is commensurable). What Aristotle is claiming here is that things (such as *the diagonal's being commensurable*) that never are could not possibly be: they are not capable of 'being and not being'. This implies that if there were never any souls, it would be impossible for there to be souls.

He holds, then, that if there is nothing able to count, then it is impossible for there to be anything able to count. This explains why, in premiss (iii), he is happy to say 'if it is *impossible* for there to be something to do the counting . . . ', where we might expect him to say 'if there *is* nothing to do the counting . . . '. On his view, the conclusion that can be drawn from (iii) (the conclusion that if it is impossible for there to be things able to count, it is impossible for there to be time) itself implies the more radical conclusion that if there *is* nothing able to count, then it is impossible for there to be time.[16]

COUNTABLES AND COUNTERS

I have claimed that Aristotle himself accepts the argument that time depends on the soul and that in doing so, he is not making a simple logical mistake. But in order to understand the argument, we need to see why he believes the crucial premiss. Why does he think that the fact that time is countable shows that it depends for its existence on beings that are able to count?

There is reason to think he would reject the *general* claim: something that is ϕ-able can only exist if there are beings able to ϕ. He says, for instance, that in a world without perceivers, the things that cause perception would still exist: 'that the subjects (*hupokeimena*) which cause the perception should not exist even without perception is impossible'.[17] The things that cause seeing and hearing are, on his view, colours and sounds.[18] So he is saying that in a world without perceivers grass would still be green, though it would not be causing anyone to see

---

[16] If it is impossible for there to be anything able to count, it is impossible for there to be time. If there is nothing able to count, it is impossible for there to be anything able to count. So: if there is nothing able to count, it is impossible for there to be time.

[17] *Metaphysics* IV. 5.1010^{b}33–5.

[18] *De Anima* II.7 (especially 418^{a}26–^{b}2, 419^{a}13–^{b}2) and II.12.424^{a}22–4.

green, and waves would still murmur, though no one would be there to hear them. Colours are visible, but they can exist even if there are no beings able to see them. Sounds are audible, but there can still be sound even if there is no one able to hear it.[19] But if he does not subscribe to the general principle that something that is ϕ-able can only exist if there are beings able to ϕ, why does he think that the fact that time is countable shows that it depends for its existence on beings that are able to count? Why doesn't he conclude (as indeed Aquinas thinks he does) that 'just as there can be sensible things, when no sense power exists, and intelligible things when no intellect exists, likewise there can be number and countable things when no one who counts exists'?[20] There are, I think, two possible answers. The first attributes to Aristotle a different general principle, for which there is some evidence in his other writings. The second depends only on his views about the way in which time is countable.

THE FIRST ANSWER: TIME IS ESSENTIALLY COUNTABLE

An important difference between time on the one hand and colours and sounds on the other is that time is essentially countable whereas colours and sounds are not essentially perceptible. There is some reason to believe that Aristotle thought that something that was *essentially* ϕ-able could not exist in a world without ϕ-ers.

Evidence for this view can be found in the passage in the *Metaphysics* in which he discusses whether there could be perceptible things if there were no animate beings.[21] Though, as I have already mentioned, he says that things, like colours and sounds, that cause perception could still exist in a world without perceivers, he adds, crucially, that in such a world they would not be perceptible. If there were no perceivers,

---

[19] This interpretation is controversial. It is defended by Broadie (1993: 137–60). For an alternative interpretation see Modrak (1987: 29–30, 46–8) and Irwin (1988: 313–14, 591–2).

[20] Aquinas, *In Phys.* Lecture 23, 629.

[21] Here I again follow Sarah Broadie's interpretation (1993: 137–60).

'perhaps it is true that there would not be perceptible things (*ta aisthēta*) nor perceptions (for they are the affections of the perceiver)' (*Metaphysics* IV.5.1010^{b}31–3). The reason why colours and sounds could nevertheless exist in a world without perceivers is that (according to Aristotle) they are not *essentially* perceptible.[22]

The claim that colour is not essentially perceptible is implied by Aristotle's more general views about definitional priority. It cannot be part of the definition of a colour that it is perceptible. Colours are what cause seeing. Sight is a passive capacity to be affected by the objects of sight (*De Anima*, 416^{b}33–5, 417^{b}19–21). According to Aristotle, a capacity to ϕ is always defined with reference to ϕ-ing. Sight, being a passive capacity, is defined with reference to seeing. But, Aristotle thinks, the activity, seeing, must be defined with reference to its objects (415^{a}20–2). To explain what seeing is we must refer to the proper objects of sight, namely colours (418^{a}11–13). It follows that colours, though they have the power to cause seeing, cannot simply be defined as things that have this power. If we refer to colours in the definition of seeing, we cannot also refer to seeing in the definition of colours.[23]

I have argued that Aristotle thinks that colours would not be perceptible in a world without perceivers. There is, then, some reason to think that he subscribes to the general principle that something ϕ-able would not be ϕ-able in a world without beings able to ϕ. From this it would follow that something that was essentially ϕ-able could not exist in such a world. Time, since it is essentially countable, depends for its existence on beings able to count.

In fact, when properly drawn, the analogy between perception and counting supports the view that time depends on the soul. This is because in drawing such an analogy, we should be comparing

---

[22] He refers to this view that colour is not essentially visible in the course of explaining his account of change in *Physics* III. He explains the distinction he draws there between *being bronze* and *being potentially something* by comparing it to the distinction between being a colour and being a visible thing: colour, he says, 'is not the same as visible thing' (*Physics* III.1.201^{b}4).

[23] Aristotle makes this clear in a passage in the *Metaphysics*. He argues that we cannot define sight by saying that it is of what is visible. 'Visible' just means 'what sight is of', so defining sight in terms of the visible is like defining sight as 'what is of what sight is of'. Instead, he claims that we should say that sight is of colour. His point is that it is better to say that sight is of colour, since we can define colour independently of sight (*Metaphysics* V. 1021^{a}33–^{b}3). See the helpful discussion in Johansen (1998: 37–8).

sight (the passive power) to countability and we should be comparing colour (the thing that has the power to cause seeing) to intellective souls. There could not be sight unless there was seeing, and there could not be seeing unless there were colours. Similarly, there could not be countability unless there was counting and there could not be counting unless there was something that had the ability to count. If there were no counters, change might exist, but the *countable aspect of change* could not.

THE SECOND ANSWER: FOR TIME TO BE COUNTABLE, IT MUST BE COUNTED

I have presented some evidence that Aristotle subscribes to a general principle that things that are essentially ϕ-able can only exist if there are beings able to ϕ. But his argument *need* not depend upon this general principle. It is possible to provide an alternative defence that appeals only to considerations about number and countability. There is, I want to argue, something about the way in which time is countable that implies that it can only be countable if there are beings able to count it.

To understand why this is so, it is necessary to recall some of our conclusions from earlier chapters. As we have seen, time, though countable, is not the kind of number with which we count. We count change (and hence time) by counting nows. When we count a now, we mark a potential division in all the changes that are going on at that now. To do this is to divide the changes into countable parts. It is in virtue of our counting that change is, in this sense, countable.

In general, of course, the fact that something is countable does not imply that it is ever actually counted. To say that something is countable is just to say that it is *such as to be counted*. A group of six pebbles, lying on the beach, is a countable collection, whether or not anyone ever counts it. However, continuous things only become countable when they are divided up into sections. Prior to such division, the most that can be said of them is that they can be *made into* something countable.

We can make a line into something countable without actually counting it. We can mark divisions on the line and then choose whether or not to go back and count the parts of the line that we have marked out. But change, unlike a line, is 'always different and different'. We cannot mark divisions in a change and then go back and count the periods that we have marked out. Instead, we have to count the divisions as we make them. For change, then, being countable implies being counted. The very act that makes a change countable is the act of counting it.[24]

If there were no ensouled beings, there would be nothing that could mark out countable parts in changes. In that case, change would not merely be uncounted; it would be uncountable. This is the reason why there can only be a *number* of change if there are beings that are able to count it.

It is instructive to compare the solution I have proposed here to one suggested in the second century AD by Alexander of Aphrodisias. Alexander argues that time, in itself, is not composed of parts. It is uniform and partless. When we, in thought, divide it into parts—into years, days, minutes, etc.—we are *creating* divisions that were not there prior to our counting. Thus, after announcing that he will 'speak of time according to the opinion of Aristotle, without disagreeing with him on any point', he writes:

Time is a single connected continuum, and is a number only because it is many in thought. For times only exist in potentiality and thought, not by being in actuality. And indeed we say that the length of a thing which is continuous, such as a long piece of wood, is such-and-such, in cubits, when it is not divided in actuality.[25]

As an account of what Aristotle thinks, this is partly right and partly wrong. Aristotle does share Alexander's view that there is a sense in which an undifferentiated continuum has no parts. When we count the before and afters in changes, we do introduce into these changes potential divisions that were not there prior to our counting. Alexander is right to say that it is because there would be no such potential divisions that there could be no time in a world without ensouled beings. But what he misses is that time, for Aristotle, is not an entity

---

[24] Of course, there could be a countable *plurality of changes*, whether or not there was any counting. But as I argued in Ch. 5, when Aristotle says that time is a number of change, he does not mean that it is a plurality of changes. Rather, it is something we count when we count changes by making, and counting, potential divisions in them. Change can only be countable in this sense, if it is in fact counted.

[25] Alexander *On Time* 94.23 in Sharples (1982).

that is already there as a uniform continuum prior to our counting. On Aristotle's view, the unity of time depends upon our counting. By our counting we do indeed create potential divisions and the change-parts that they delimit, but it is only because we create these change-parts that changes can all be arranged in a single before and after order. That is why time is essentially countable.[26]

This conclusion about the role of counting follows from views I attributed to Aristotle earlier in the book. I have argued that, for Aristotle, time is what we count by counting nows as they pass. If there were no counting, there could still be changes, each with its own before and after order. And there would still be certain time-*like* relations between these changes. There would be a *kind* of relation of simultaneity: some changes would be going on *while* others were going on. And there would also be certain relations of precedence between changes simply in virtue of the fact that some of them gave rise to others. Whether or not there was any counting, there would be a sense in which the coming to be of a parent preceded the coming to be of its child.[27] Moreover, if there were no counting, it might even be true that certain changes were past and others were yet to come.[28]

But none of this, on Aristotle's view, amounts to there being time. These time-*like* relations of simultaneity and precedence can only be fully temporal if they are associated with a before and after series of nows. And again, it is only because there is such a before and after series that it is possible for there to be *a* past (in the sense of a series of times stretching further and further into the past) and *a* future (in the sense of a series of times stretching further and further into the future).[29] By counting a before and after series of nows, we divide changes into

---

[26] If this is right, it raises a question about whether Aristotle can consistently hold that there is a temporal before and after that stretches into the future. As we have seen, his view is that we count changes *as they occur*: we count a now, and in so doing make a potential division in any change that is going on. This implies that future changes have not yet been counted. So *they* are not yet divided into simultaneous countable parts in the way that I have argued they must be if they are to form a single before and after order. This is a difficulty that Aristotle never acknowledges. It suggests that he is committed to the view that there is, in a sense, no future time: there is no single before and after order stretching further and further into the future. But if that is so, in what sense does the now unite the past with the future?

[27] As I explained in Ch. 4, p. 81.

[28] As I suggested in Ch. 8, n. 7.

[29] See Ch. 8, pp. 127–8.

exactly simultaneous countable parts. As I argued in Chapter 7, it is necessary that changes have such parts if time is to be a universal order within which all changes are related to each other.[30]

This explains why the notions of counting and countability are so central to Aristotle's view of time. It is our counting that creates the ordered series of nows. These nows mark potential divisions in *all* the changes that are going on at them. Without these counted nows, there would be no single before and after order within which all changes were arranged. Without them, that is, there would be no time.

[30] Ch. 7, pp. 115–16.

APPENDIX

The Expression *'Ho pote on X esti'*

The expression *ho pote on X esti* occurs only rarely in Aristotle. He uses it in several places in his account of time, but apart from this, he only uses it on two occasions: twice in a passage in the *Parts of Animals* (649^{a}15–16, 649^{b}24–5) and once in the *Generation and Corruption* (319^{b}3–4). There is little agreement on how it should be understood. I shall first explain the linguistic possibilities and then ask which of these possibilities makes best sense of the contexts in which the expression is employed in Aristotle's account of time.

THE LINGUISTIC POSSIBILITIES

The Syntax

To simplify matters, let us consider only the expression *ho on X esti*. It will help us to understand the syntax of this expression if we substitute a variable for the pronoun *ho*. It then becomes: *Y on X esti*. There are two basic ways to construe this, depending on whether X is the subject or the complement of *esti*:

(i) X, by (or by virtue of) being Y, is.

(ii) By (or by virtue of) being Y, [something or other which is given by the context] is X.

There are, moreover, three different possible versions of (i), depending on whether we understand the 'is' as (a) 'exists', (b) 'is what it is' (i.e. is X) or (c) 'is [something or other given by the context]'.[1]

The Word *pote*

How should we translate the word *pote*? Again, there are two linguistic possibilities. It could have a temporal sense, meaning 'at any time' or 'at any given

---

[1] I would like to thank Edward Hussey for helping me to see clearly what the alternatives are here.

moment'.[2] Or it could have the sense of the English word 'whatever'.[3] *Pote* has this non-temporal sense in a relative clause in the *Theaetetus* (160e): 'this is what our efforts have brought forth whatever it really is' (*hoti de pote tugchanei on*). This second, non-temporal sense is, I think, more likely in the context of Aristotle's account of time. To take the *pote* in its temporal sense makes nonsense, for instance, of his use of this expression at 223ᵃ27, where he writes of *touto ho pote on estin ho chronos*. If the '*pote*' here were temporal, he would be writing of how time was *at a time*.

The two ways to understand the expression are thus:

(i) X by virtue of being Y (whatever that is) is.[4]

(ii) By being Y (whatever that is), [something or other] is X.

THE MEANING OF THIS EXPRESSION IN THE CONTEXT
OF ARISTOTLE'S ACCOUNT OF TIME

The expression occurs in four different types of context in Aristotle's account of time.[5] First, at 219ᵃ20–1, Aristotle says that the before and after in a *kinēsis* is *ho men pote on kinēsis estin*, but its being (*einai*) is different and not change. Second, Aristotle says (twice) that though the now is different, *ho de pote on esti to nun* is the same (219ᵇ14–15, 219ᵇ26). Third, he tells us that the thing-in-motion (*pheromenon*) is different in *logos*, but *touto de ho men pote on* is the same (219ᵇ18–19). Again, he says that the thing-in-motion makes the motion one by being the same, and explains that by this, he does not mean the same '*ho pote on*, for that might leave a gap but [the same] in *logos*' (220ᵃ7–8). Finally, he says that if there were no ensouled beings, there would be no time, but there might be *touto ho pote on estin ho chronos*, if it was possible for there to be change in the absence of soul (223ᵃ26–8).

In none of these places is there any obvious subject for *esti* that can be supplied from the context, other than the X in the phrase *ho pote on X esti*. For

---

[2] It is translated in this way by Bostock (1980: 150).

[3] This is how Hussey understands it (1993: 148).

[4] On this interpretation, the neuter participle *on* sometimes has a feminine subject. For instance, at 219ᵃ20–1, the subject of the participle would be *kinēsis*. Brague (1982) (who defends this interpretation) translates these lines as follows: 'the before and after in change is that, whatever it is, being which change is what it is'. As Brague points out, it is possible, when the predicate is a substantive with *einai*, for the participle to agree by attraction with the predicate substantive nearest to it (in this case, the pronoun *ho*). He gives examples of this in (1982: 103 n. 10).

[5] I shall discuss later the expression *ho pot' ēn*, at 219ᵇ11.

this reason, the most plausible way to take the expression here is in sense (i).[6] In other words, *ho* is the complement of the participle *on* and the subject of *esti* is the X in the schema *ho pote on X esti*.

The expression *X esti* should, I think, be understood here as 'X is what it is' (i.e. in sense (b) above). 'X exists' (sense (a)) is also a possible translation, but it does not capture so well the point Aristotle is making. In these passages, he is interested primarily in the grounds for X's being what it is (though of course, these are also, in a sense, grounds for X's existence as the kind of thing it is). The suggestion that *X esti* should be understood in sense (c), as 'X is [something or other supplied by the context]', can be dismissed because the contexts in question do not supply obvious complements for *esti*.

The relevant passages should, then, be translated:

The before and after in a change is that, whatever it is, by being which a change is, but its being is different and not change.   (219[a]20–1)

That, whatever it is, by being which the now is is the same.   (219[b]14–15 and similarly at 219[b]26)

That, whatever it is, by being which the thing-in-motion is is the same.   (219[b]18–19)

The thing-in-motion makes the motion one by being one (and not because that, whatever it is, by being which it is is one, for that might leave a gap, but one in *logos*).   (220[a]7–8)

There would be no time without the soul, except that there might be that, whatever it is, by being which time is.   (223[a]26–8)

This explains how the expression should be translated. But what exactly does it mean? For this, it is necessary to look to the interpretation I have given of the various passages in which it occurs. But there are, I think, two general points that can usefully be made here.

First, it is very unlikely that, when he uses the phrase *ho pote on X esti*, Aristotle simply means the *hupokeimenon* of X (i.e. its subject, or underlying thing).[7] There is nothing about the meaning of the phrase that suggests that it

---

[6] In understanding the expression in this way I am following Brague (1982). Torstrik also explains the expression in this way (1857: esp. 170–3), but though he construes the phrase as Brague does, he nevertheless maintains that it simply means 'in substrate'. Compare also Charles (2004). Charles follows Brague in his interpretation of the expression *ho pote on*, but his conclusions about Aristotle's view of the now are quite different from mine.

[7] Both Philoponos and Simplicius interpret the phrase in this way. For example, Philoponos, in discussing the occurrence of the phrase at 219[a]20–1, writes: 'the before and after *kata to hupokeimenon* (for this he calls '*ho pote on*') is nothing other than

refers to the *hupokeimenon*. If that were all Aristotle meant, it would be unnecessary for him to introduce this unusual expression at all. Second, he makes it clear that he means to distinguish between *ho pote on X esti* and the *einai* or *logos* of X. For example, he tells us that the before and after in change is that, whatever it is, by being which change is, but its *being* is different and not change (219ᵃ19–21). And again, in his account of the now he says that the now is different in being (*einai*) but that *that, whatever it is, by being which the now is* is the same (219ᵇ26–7). He makes the distinction again in a remark about the thing-in-motion: for the thing-in-motion to make the movement one it is not enough for *that, whatever it is, by being which it is* to remain the same; it must remain the same in *logos* (220ᵃ7–8). Finally, in lines 223ᵃ27–8, he implies that *that by being which time is* is change (or possibly the before and after in change), but we already know that time is not identical to change (or even to the before and after in change). It is a mistake, then, to take *ho pote on X esti* to mean: 'what X really is'.

Ho pote on X esti is, I think, something that is not identical with X but is in some sense a ground or basis for the being of X. On the interpretation I have suggested, the participle *'on'* must be some kind of circumstantial participle. The only kind of circumstantial participle it can be in this context is a participle with explanatory force. With the phrase '*ho pote on X esti*', Aristotle picks out something in a very abstract way. In order for this phrase to be picking out anything that is worth mentioning, there must be a close connection between X and *ho pote on X esti*. The connection cannot, in the context of the discussion of time, be that X is contemporaneous with *ho pote on X esti*. It must, then, be that *ho pote on X esti* is something that provides the ground for X's being what it is.

We can now look back at the places in which this expression occurs in Aristotle's account of time. At 219ᵃ20–1, Aristotle says that that by being which change is is the before and after in change.[8] If I am right about the meaning of this, then he is implying that the before and after in a change provides an explanatory ground for the change's being the change it is. As I argued in Chapter 4, it provides the structure of the change.[9] At 219ᵇ19, after saying that *ho pote on the thing-in-motion is* is the same, Aristotle adds 'for it is point or stone or something else of this kind'. So, for example, that by being which the stone-in-motion is is the stone. The stone is not identical with the

---

change'. (Philoponos, *In Phys.* 720, 27–8; Simplicius, *In Phys.* 726, 20–1.) Franco Volpi (1988: 33), who understands the phrase in this way, claims that *ho pote on* is short for *ho pote tugchanei on hupokeimenon*. Some support for this interpretation is provided by Aristotle's use of the phrase '*ho men gar pote tugchanei on to hupokeimenon*' at *Parts of Animals* 649ᵃ15.

[8] Ross's reasons for bracketing *estin* are, I think, insufficient (Ross 1936: 598).
[9] Ch. 4, pp. 65–6.

stone-in-motion, but it is a ground for the being of the stone-in-motion. At 219^{b}26–7, he says that that by being which the now is is the same, and then adds: 'for it is the before and after in change'. Again, the before and after in change is not identical to the now, but it is the ground for the being of the now. As Aristotle goes on to say, it is because the before and after in change is countable, that the now is what it is (219^{b}28). Finally, at 223^{a}26–9, he argues that that by being which time is might exist without the soul, and supports this by saying that change might exist without the soul. This suggests that change (or perhaps the before and after in change) is that by being which time is. And change is, indeed, related to time in the way we would expect it to be if it is that by being which time is. It is not identical to time, but it is a basis for time's being what it is. Time is, as we have seen, a number of change.

THE EXPRESSION *to gar nun* TO AUTO HO POT' ĒN AT 219^{b}10–11

Since the phrase, *to gar nun to auto ho pot' ēn* (219^{b}10–11) does not have a participle, *on*, it should not be translated, on the model of our interpretation of *ho pote on X esti*, as 'that, whatever it is, by being which the now is is the same'. Instead, I think, Aristotle is simply saying here that 'the now (whichever now it is) is the same'. He presents this as an explanation of the fact that all simultaneous time is the same.[10] His point is that the times of simultaneous changes are all bounded by one and the same now.

He goes on to say that this now is different in being (219^{b}11). If my interpretation is right, then he is not here saying that *earlier and later* nows are different in being, but rather that the one now that divides all simultaneous changes is itself different in being. What could he mean by this? He must, I think, have in mind the fact that one and the same now can be described in terms of any of the changes it bounds. Suppose that at one and the same instant I wake up and someone fires a gun. This instant can be described either as the instant of my waking up or as the instant of the gun's being fired. These instants are (numerically) the same, but we can also distinguish between the instant *qua* instant of my waking up and the instant *qua* instant of the gun's being fired. The instant of my waking up and the instant of the gun's being fired are one and the same instant, but there is a sense in which they are different in being.[11]

---

[10] I discuss this claim in Ch. 7, above.

[11] My interpretation here is suggested by Ross's paraphrase (1936: 598): 'the time of one event is identical with the time of another simultaneous event; for the now involved, whatever now it may have been, is identical (though it is one thing for it to be the now involved in the time of one event, and another thing to be the now involved in the time of another simultaneous event)'.

Bibliography

Standard editions of the works of Plato and Aristotle have been used throughout.

ANNAS, J. 1975. 'Aristotle, Number and Time', *The Philosophical Quarterly* 25: 97–113.

—— 1976. *Aristotle's Metaphysics. Books Mu and Nu*. Translation and commentary. Clarendon Aristotle Series. Oxford.

—— 1984. 'Die Gegenstände der Mathematik bei Aristoteles', in A. Graeser (ed.), *Mathematics and Metaphysics in Aristotle*. Papers of the Tenth Symposium Aristotelicum. Bern and Stuttgart, pp. 131–47.

AQUINAS, ST THOMAS. 1965. *S. Thomae Aquinatis In Octo Libros Physicorum Aristotelis Expositio*, ed. P. M. Maggliòlo. Turin.

BARNES, J. 1980. 'Aristotle and the Methods of Ethics', *Revue Internationale de Philosophie* 34: 490–511.

—— 1984. *The Complete Works of Aristotle. The Revised Oxford Translation*. 2 vols. Princeton.

—— 1985. 'Metaphysics', in J. Barnes (ed.), *Cambridge Companion to Aristotle*. Cambridge, pp. 66–108.

BARREAU, H. 1968. 'L'instant et le temps selon Aristote', *La Revue philosophique de Louvain* 66: 213–38.

—— 1973 'Le traité aristotélicien du temps', *Revue philosophique de la France et de l'étranger* 163: 401–37.

BIGELOW, J. 1996 'Presentism and Properties', *Philosophical Perspectives*, 10: 35–52.

BLACKWELL, R. J., and R. J. SPATH, and W. E. THIRLKEL. 1963. Translation of Aquinas' *Commentary on Aristotle's Physics* (with an introduction by V. J. Bourke). New Haven.

BÖHME, G. 1974. *Zeit und Zahl. Studien zur Zeittheorie bei Platon, Aristoteles, Leibniz und Kant*, in *Philosophische Abhandlungen*, 45, Frankfurt am Main.

BONITZ, H. 1870. *Index Aristotelicus*. Berlin.

BOSTOCK, D. 1980. 'Aristotle's Account of Time', *Phronesis* 25: 148–69.

—— 1991. 'Aristotle on Continuity in *Physics* VI', in L. Judson (ed.), *Aristotle's Physics: A Collection of Essays*. Oxford, pp. 179–212.

BRAGUE, R. 1982. *Du temps chez Platon et Aristote*. Paris.

BROADIE, (WATERLOW), S. 1982a. *Nature, Change and Agency in Aristotle's Physics*. Oxford.

—— 1982b *Passage and Possibility. A Study of Aristotle's Modal Concepts.* Oxford.

—— 1984. 'Aristotle's Now', *The Philosophical Quarterly* 34: 104–28.

—— 1993. 'Aristotle's Perceptual Realism', *Southern Journal of Philosophy,* Supp. *Vol., Spindel Conference 1992: Ancient Minds* 31: 137–60.

BURNYEAT, M. 1990. *The Theaetetus of Plato,* trans. M. J. Levett, Indianapolis, Cambridge.

CALLAHAN, J. F. 1948. *Four Views of Time in Ancient Philosophy.* Cambridge.

CARTERON, H. 1924. 'Remarques sur la notion de temps d'après Aristote', *Revue philosophique de la France et de l'étranger* 98: 67–81.

CHARLES, D. 2004. 'GC1.5: Simple Genesis and Prime Matter', in F. de Haas and J. Mansfeld (eds.), *Aristotle: On Generation and Corruption I. Symposium Aristotelicum.* Oxford, pp. 151–69.

COLIN, B. 1993. *Aristote Physica. Index verborum: Listes de fréquence.* Liège.

COLLOBERT, C. 1994. *Aristote. Traité du Temps. Physique, Livre IV, 10–14.* Introduction, traduction et commentaire. Paris.

CONEN, P. F. 1952. 'Aristotle's Definition of Time', *The New Scholasticism* 26: 441–58.

—— 1964. *Die Zeittheorie des Aristoteles.* Zetemata, Monographien zur klassischen Altertumswissenschaft 35. Munich.

COOPE, U. C. M. 2001. 'Why does Aristotle say that there is no Time without Change?' *Proceedings of the Aristotelian Society* 101/3: 359–67.

COOPER, J. M. (ed.) 1997. *Plato: Complete Works* (Associate editor, D. S. Hutchinson). Indianapolis, Indiana.

CORISH, D. 1976. 'Aristotle's attempted Derivation of Temporal Order from that of Movement and Space', *Phronesis* 21: 241–51.

DEHN, M. 1975. 'Raum, Zeit, Zahl bei Aristoteles vom mathematischen Standpunkt aus', in G. A. Seeck (ed.), *Die Naturphilosophie des Aristoteles.* Darmstadt, pp. 199–218. (Originally in *Scientia. Rivista internazionale di sintesi scientifica* 60 (1936): 12–21, 69–74.)

DESTRÉE, P. 1991. 'Le nombre et la perception. Note sur la définition Aristotélicienne du temps', *Revue de Philosophie Ancienne* 9: 59–81.

DUBOIS, J. M. 1967. *Le Temps et l'Instant selon Aristote (Physique, IV, 10–14).* Paris.

DUHEM, P. 1913–59. *Le Système du monde; histoire des doctrines cosmologiques de Platon à Copernic.* Paris.

EUCLID. 1978. *Eukleidou Stoicheia. Euclide; texte grec et traduction francaise libre,* ed. G. J. Kayas, Paris.

FESTUGIÈRE, A. J. 1934. 'Le temps et l'âme selon Aristote', *Revue des sciences philosophiques et théologiques* 23: 5–28.

FINE, K. 1994. 'Essence and Modality', *Philosophical Perspectives* 8: 1–16.

GHINS, M. 1991. 'Two Difficulties with Regard to Aristotle's Treatment of Time', *Revue de Philosophie Ancienne* 9: 83–98.

GOLDSCHMIDT, V. 1982. *Temps Physique et Temps Tragique chez Aristote, commentaire sur le quatrième livre de la Physique (10–14) et sur la Poétique.* Paris.

HASPER, P. S. 2003. 'The Metaphysics of Continuity. Zeno, Democritus and Aristotle'. Dissertation, Rijksuniversiteit Groningen.

HEATH, T. L. 1921. *A History of Greek Mathematics.* Oxford.

HEINAMAN, R 1994. 'Is Aristotle's Definition of Change Circular?', *Apeiron* 27: 25–37.

—— 1987. 'Aristotle and the Identity of Actions', *History of Philosophy Quarterly* 4: 307–28.

HUSSEY, E. 1993. *Aristotle's Physics Books III and IV.* Translated with an introduction and notes. Oxford.

INWOOD, M. 1991. 'Aristotle on the Reality of Time', in L. Judson (ed.), *Aristotle's Physics: A Collection of Essays.* Oxford, pp. 151–78.

IRWIN, T. H. 1988. *Aristotle's First Principles.* New York.

JOHANSEN, T. K. 1998. *Aristotle on the Sense-organs.* Cambridge.

JUDSON, L. 1983. 'Eternity and Necessity in *De Caelo* I.12', *Oxford Studies in Ancient Philosophy* 1: 217–55.

—— (ed.) 1991. *Aristotle's Physics: A Collection of Essays.* Oxford.

KING, R. A. H. 2001. *Aristotle on Life and Death.* London.

KLEIN, J. 1968. *Greek Mathematical Thought and the Origins of Algebra.* Cambridge, Mass. and London.

KOSMAN, L. A. 1969. 'Aristotle's Definition of Motion', *Phronesis* 14: 40–62.

KOSTMAN, J. 1987. 'Aristotle's Definition of Change', *History of Philosophy Quarterly* 4: 3–16.

KUHLMANN, H. 1988. ' "Jetzt"? Zur Konzeption des nun in der Zeitabhandlung des Aristoteles (Physik, IV, 10–14)', in E. Rudolph (ed.), *Zeit, Bewegung, Handlung. Studien zur Zeitabhandlung des Aristoteles,* Stuttgart, pp. 63–96.

LEAR, J. 1982. 'Aristotle's Philosophy of Mathematics', *The Philosophical Review* 91: 161–92.

LEGGATT, S. 1995. *Aristotle: On the Heavens I and II.* Warminster.

LEWIS, D. 1976. 'The Paradoxes of Time Travel', *American Philosophical Quarterly* 13: 145–52.

LUCAS, J. R. 1973. *A Treatise on Time and Space.* London.

MAUDLIN, T. 2002. 'Remarks on the Passing of Time', *Proceedings of the Aristotelian Society* 102/3: 237–52.

McTAGGART, J. M. E. 1968. *The Nature of Existence.* Grosse Pointe, Mich.

MELLOR, D. H. 1998. *Real Time II.* London and New York.

MIGNUCCI, M. 1984. 'Aristotle's Arithmetic', in G. A. Graeser (ed.), *Mathematics and Metaphysics in Aristotle*. Papers of the Tenth Symposium Aristotelicum. Berne and Stuttgart, pp. 175–211.

MILLER, F. D. 1974. 'Aristotle on the Reality of Time', *Archiv für Geschichte der Philosophie* 56: 132–55.

MODRAK, D. 1987. *Aristotle the Power of Perception*. Chicago.

MOREAU, J. 1965. *L'Espace et le Temps selon Aristote*. Padua.

MORISON, B. 2002 *On Location. Aristotle's Concept of Place*. Oxford.

MOST, G. W. 1988. 'Ein Problem in der aristotelischen Zeitabhandlung', in E. Rudolph (ed.), *Zeit, Bewegung, Handlung. Studien zur Zeitabhandlung des Aristoteles*. Stuttgart, pp. 11–25.

NEWTON-SMITH, W. H. 1980. *The Structure of Time*. London.

OWEN, G. E. L. 1961. '*Tithenai ta phainomena*', in S. Mansion (ed.), *Aristote et les problèmes de méthode*. Papers of the Second Symposium Aristotelicum. Louvain, pp. 83–103. (Reprinted in Martha Nussbaum (ed.), *Logic, Science and Dialectic*. Ithaca, NY, 1986, pp. 239–51.)

—— 1966 'Plato and Parmenides on the Timeless Present', *The Monist* 50: 317–40. (Reprinted in Martha Nussbaum (ed.), *Logic, Science and Dialectic*. Ithaca, NY, 1986, pp. 27–44.)

—— 1970. 'Aristotle: Method, Physics and Cosmology', in *Dictionary of Scientific Biography*, ed. C. C. Gillespie, volume 1, pp. 250–8. New York. (Reprinted in Martha Nussbaum (ed.), *Logic, Science and Dialectic*. Ithaca, NY, 1986, pp. 151–64).

—— 1976. 'Aristotle on Time', in P. Machamer and R. Turnbull (eds.), *Motion and Time, Space and Matter*. Columbus, pp. 3–27. (Reprinted in Martha Nussbaum (ed.), *Logic, Science and Dialectic*. Ithaca, NY, 1986, pp. 295–314.)

PHILOPONOS. 1888. *Ioannis Philoponi In Aristotelis Physicorum Libros V Posteriores Commentaria*, ed. Hieronymus Vitelli. Berlin.

PLOTINUS. 1967. *Enneads*, trans. and ed. A. H. Armstrong. Loeb Classical Library. London.

PRICE, H. 1996. *Time's Arrow and Archimedes' Point. New Directions for the Physics of Time*. Oxford.

PRITCHARD, P. 1995. *Plato's Philosophy of Mathematics*. Sankt Augustin.

ROSS, W. D. 1936. *Aristotle's Physics*, a revised text with introduction and commentary, Oxford.

RUDOLPH, E. (ed.) 1988. *Zeit, Bewegung, Handlung. Studien zur Zeitabhandlung des Aristoteles*. Forschungen und Berichte der Evangelischen Studiengemeinschaft, v.42. Stuttgart.

RUSSELL, B. 1937. *Principles of Mathematics*. New York.

—— 1981. 'Mathematics and the Metaphysicians', reprinted in *Mysticism and Logic and Other Essays*. Totowa, NJ.

SCHLESINGER, G. N. 1982. 'How Time Flies', *Mind* 91: 501–23.

SEECK, G. A. 1975. *Die Naturphilosophie des Aristoteles*. Darmstadt.

—— 1987. 'Zeit als Zahl bei Aristoteles', *Rheinisches Museum für Philologie* 130: 107–24.

SHARPLES, R. in collaboration with F. W. Zimmermann. 1982. 'Alexander of Aphrodisias, *On Time*' (A translation from the Latin with notes on the Arabic text). *Phronesis* 27: 58–81.

SHOEMAKER, S. S. 1969. 'Time without Change', *Journal of Philosophy* 66: 363–81.

SIMPLICIUS. 1882. *Simplicii In Aristotelis Physicorum Libros IV Priores Commentaria*, ed. Hermann Diels. Berlin.

SMART, J. J. C. 1949. 'The River of Time', *Mind* 58: 483–94.

SMYTH, H. W. 1956. *Greek Grammar*. Cambridge, Mass.

SORABJI, R. 1980. *Necessity, Cause and Blame*. London.

—— 1983. *Time, Creation and the Continuum*. London.

THEMISTIUS. 1900. *In Aristotelis Physica paraphrasis*, ed. Henricus Schenkl. Berlin.

TORSTRIK, A. 1857. 'Ho pote on. Ein Beitrag zur Kenntnis des aristotelischen Sprachgebrauchs', *Rheinisches Museum für Philologie* 12: 161–73.

—— 1867. 'Über die Abhandlung des Aristoteles von der Zeit, Phys. D 10ff.', *Philologus* 26: 446–523.

URMSON, J. O. 1992. Translation of Simplicius' *On Aristotle's Physics 4.1–5, 10–14*. (Introduction and appendix by R. Sorabji.) Ithaca, NY.

VLASTOS, G. 1965a. 'The Disorderly Motion in the *Timaeus*', in R. E. Allen (ed.), *Studies in Plato's Metaphysics*. New York, pp. 379–99. (Originally in *Classical Quarterly* 33 (1939): 71–83.)

—— 1965b. 'Creation in the "Timaeus": Is it a Fiction?', in R. E. Allen (ed.), *Studies in Plato's Metaphysics*. New York, pp. 401–19.

VOLPI, F. 1988. 'Chronos und Psyche. Die aristotelische Aporie von Physik IV, 14, 223^{a}16–29', in E. Rudolph (ed.), *Zeit, Bewegung, Handlung. Studien zur Zeitabhandlung des Aristoteles*. Stuttgart, pp. 26–62.

WAGNER, H. 1967. *Aristoteles Physikvorlesung*. Berlin.

WIELAND, W. 1970. *Die aristotelische Physik*. Göttingen.

WILLIAMS, D. C. 1951. 'The Myth of Passage', *Journal of Philosophy* 48: 457–72.

ZELLER, E. 1878. *Aristoteles und die alten Peripatetiker, Die Philosophie der Griechen in ihrer geschichtlichen Entwicklung dargestellt*. Berlin.

Index Locorum

General Index

distinguished from mere
  analogy 48–9, 55, 72–5
  explains how time can measure
  change 109
Goldschmidt, V. 160 n. 5
hama (together, simultaneous) 114
  n. 4, 122–3; *see also*
  simultenaeity
Harold, King 65–6
Hasper, P. S. 22 n. 11
Heath, T. L. 88 n. 6
heavenly bodies, *see* celestial motions
Heinaman, R. 6 n. 17
Heraclitus' posset 137
ho pote on X esti 66, 114–5 n. 5,
  126–9, 133–9, 159, 173–7
  distinct from expression *ho pote*
  ēn 114–5 n. 5, 177
Homer 153
Hussey, E. 6 n. 17, 9, 40–1, 48 n. 3,
  52 n. 11, 89 n. 10, 92, 96 n.
  24, 114–5 n. 5, 117 n. 9, 128
  n. 9, 132 n. 17, 134 n. 23,
  137 n. 31, 149 n. 18, 173
  n. 1, 174 n. 3
Hutchinson, D. S. 32 n. 4

infinite 2–3, 9–11, 17, 51–2, 89 n. 10
  changes 51 n. 10, 75–7
  divisibility 2–3, 9–11, 28–30,
    51–3, 55–9, 115
  qualitative changes only
    accidentally infinitely
    divisible, 52, 56 n. 21
  see also continuity; divisions
  series of generations 81
  time 51 n. 10, 80 n. 29, 109 n.17,
    146–7
  see also celestial motion

Inwood, M. 20 n. 6
Irwin, T. H. 167 n. 19

Johansen, T. K. 168 n. 23
Judson, L. 154 n. 26

kinēsis, *see* change
Klein, J. 90 n. 13, 120 n. 14
Kosman, L. A. 6 n. 17
Kostman, J. 6 n. 17

Leggatt, S. 154 n. 26
Lewis, D. 79–80 n. 28
logos, sameness in 126, 137

magnitude (*megethos*)
  analogous with change 9, 72–5,
    77–9
  before and after in 60, 67–9
  means spatially extended
    magnitude 47, 50–1
  measurement of continuous
    magnitude 100–3
  prior to change 53–4, 77–9
  see also before and after; continuity;
    following
Maudlin, T. 37 n. 16
McTaggart, J. M. E. 128 n. 8
measure
  being in time and being measured
    by time 152–3
  not the same as number 87, 96–8,
    99–104
  the now measures change 97
  time measures change and vice
    versa 104–9
  and units 99–109
Mellor, D. H. 4 n. 14, 148 n. 14
method, Aristotle's 17, 31–2,
  f37–41
Mignucci, M. 164–6

triangle, sameness and difference
  of 118–20

unit 86, 101–9, 127
universe
  uniqueness of 33–4
  view that sphere of universe is
    time 31 n. 2
  see also celestial motions

Vlastos, G. 109 n. 17, 146 n. 8
void 2 n. 8, 57 n. 22
Volpi, F. 175–6 n. 7

Wagner, H. 113 n. 1
waterfall illusion 63 n. 4
Williams, D. C. 3 n. 12.

Xenocrates 146 n. 8

Zeller, E. 96 n. 24
Zeno 10 n. 21